JOSE RODULFO BOETA

BERNARDO DE GALVEZ

PUBLICACIONES ESPAÑOLAS
MADRID, 1977

BERNARDO DE GALVEZ

*The great protagonist of Spain's help in the
independence of the United States.*

BERNARDO DE GALVEZ AND THE BICENTENNIAL

This 18th century Andalusian gentleman, whose portrait at the head of his troops we can see in the Museum of the Army in Madrid, in a miniature in a showcase in which is preserved the English banner taken at the capture of Pensacola, is Bernardo de Gálvez, a Spaniard —soldier and man of government— who from the long frontier of the Mississippi and the bulwarks of Florida, in peace and in war, with the reserve of diplomacy, first, and the power of arms, later, contributed decisively to bring to reality the dream of liberty of the United States of America.

A telegraphic record of his endless service record could be written as follows: born in a town in the Málaga range, followed the vocation of arms, shed his blood on three continents, expelled the English from the Gulf of Mexico, assisted at the birth of a country which came to be the most powerful on earth and is buried in the capital of New Spain, where he died, still young, like a classic hero, recently named Viceroy.

Bernardo de Gálvez, Captain General of New Orleans, Governor of Louisiana and Florida, Count of Gálvez, Viceroy of Mexico, exemplary servant and executor of far-ranging policy, is the figure who personifies the help of Carlos III in the war of the American colonies, this complex chapter of the history of Spain in the 18th century, not always well understood, and at times silenced, and whose pages, some of them decisive for the revolution of the colonists, have still not achieved the recognition which, objectively, they deserve.

A simple fact serves as a touch-stone and contrast to show the quality of the conduct we have just referred to. It is know that the independence movement of the thirteen colonies of the Union, openly supported by France and Spain, against England, had two outstanding European «patrons», Paul de La Fayette and Bernardo de Gálvez. However, while the French general is considered in the United States as a national hero and the alliance with Louis XVI is exhalted as it deserves to be, Gálvez is almost unknown and the flood of Spanish aid is frequently undervalued and over-looked, or completely omitted in history books and manuals. It is not strange then that a poll recently taken should confirm that the average American is unaware not only of who was the protagonist of Spanish assistance in the struggle of his nation, but of the fact that there even was such assistance.

Now, when the Liberty Bell has rung again, evoking the beat of 1776, and the United States are celebrating the Bicentennial of their Independence, Bernardo de Gál-vez is present at the jubilant commemorations through his equestrian statue, the work of Juan de Avalos, which has been donated and inaugurated by King Juan Carlos I in Washington, «*as a permanent memory of the blood shed by Spanish soldiers in defense of the American cause*».

The Bicentennial is a good occasion, in tribute to the truth, for the facts to be known and tribute paid to the memory of a true all of America, as without his daring, capacity and decision the emancipation process of the colonies might have followed a different course. Of Ber-nardo de Gálvez (a name forgotten in the nation which he helped to liberate), the writer B. Parker Thompson has said he was the «*Hawk of Spain*» and considers him as «*the most valuable friend the United States has had in all its history*».

The dossier of the acts of Bernardo de Gálvez is found, above all, in the files and manuscripts of the Spanish archives and, also, in the parallel North American docu-mentation which is now beginning to be dug up by the historians and used as working material in the seminars of the universities and in the research departments. Let us recall that Herbert Bolton asked as a first step in bridging the gap of the lack of knowledge of the Spanish culture in North America: «*one of the greatest urgencies is the publication of all the historical material referring to the activity of the Spanish within the present borders of the United States*».

7

In the letters and diaries of Bernardo de Gálvez, in the military reports and acts, in minutes and duplicates, in the diplomatic correspondence, and in the testimony of his contemporaries, there shows itself —and we are going to follow its traces in the lines which follow— the brilliant biography of this «*Hawk of Spain*» which flew from the mountains of Macharavialla to distant horizons.

THE ESCORIAL OF THE GALVEZ

Over the abrupt spine of the mountains of Málaga, on the slope of the range, beside one of the dry reverbeds which lead to the coast, the rural settlement of Macharavialla huddles like a multi-levelled, white-washed hive. The setting is bluish-green under the intense light of the skies of Málaga and there is the sound of the beat of the seas. There crawl along the slopes almond trees, carob beans and an occasional olive grove; below, in the rich soil of the ravines, there are orchards, lemon and orange groves, thick fields of sugar cane. And vineyards. Vineyards which creep up the highest hills, carpeting the red earth. They are the remains of an ancient wealth decimated beyond salvage by blight. From these vines was distilled the finest nectar in the world, raisin must, amber and honey in color, the true virgin «*Málaga*», the wine praised by Julius Caesar, still not sophisticated in the farmhouse presses. Near Macharavialla is Benaque and, further up, crowning the half-moon of the valley like a dovecote, Benagalbón.

The visit to Macharavialla (it is a score of kilometers on the highway to Almería, later turning inland) is a continual surprise. There are flowers. White-washed walls. And these unique street names: «*New Orleans Street*», «*Mobile Plaza*», «*Pensacola Street*»... How astonishing to find such names, referring to the geography of a far continent, blended into the daily existence of a small Andalusian village, among simple people, goat-herds, craftsmen, vineyard workers, farm-hands watering their horses... These places were the scene of the shildhood of Bernardo de Gálvez; now, with their astonishing names, these hills and alleys seem to proclaim the threads of a resounding biography.

At the entrance to the town there is an old obelisk with a plaque whose worn letters read: «*Calvary erected by H. E. Don José de Gálvez in thanksging for having recovered his health*». In the upper part, where stod the rustic tower of the Gálvez family, we find the «*House of the Countess*», with evocative details, furnishings and escutcheons. The «*Countess*» is the Malaguenian writer Angeles Rubio Argüelles, Countess of Berlanga del Duero, who has tirelessly researched over many years the history of the Gálvez family, publishing many books and monographs, and has poured out her sensitivity and persistence to defend the historic past of the town, in great part discovered by her.

We stand now before the great mass of the parish church, neoclassic in style, with the arms of Carlos III on the facade over the carved entrance, and the sun dial set into one of the groins. The Archbishop of Sevilla,

Fray Diego de Deza ordered it built in 1505, and it was rebuilt in 1785 under the patronage of the Marquis of Sonora and his two brothers, under the supervision of Domínguez del Castillo. What could well be called the «*Escorial of the Gálvez*» is a spacious church, sober in its architecture. It seems to be closed, but Manolo, the pleasant owner of a nearby bar —the Bar Sonora—, where you can sip a glass, or several, of this delicious «*Málaga*» of Macharavialla which we have mentioned before, hastens to open the great door with the key and accompanies us to act as «*host*». Over the side altars and the main altar there was a valuable collection of paintings of evangelical themes by Murillo. («*The Betrothal of Our Lady*», «*St. Michael Archangel*», «*St. Anthony of Padua*», «*Ste. Anna*» and «*St. Matthew*»). Today only the blank spaces are to be seen because the paintings were burned in a great bonfire during our last Civil War. Some of the townspeople, as a consolation which links them to other times, still preserve old photographs of these paintings. On the walls may still be read plaques listing the donations made by the Gálvez family for the decoration of the church.

Had through the rear façade, next to the burial places, whose center is occupied by the sarcophagus with the ashes of Doña María Josefa de Madrid Gallardo, mother of the founders, may be admired the praying statues, in alabaster, of the most outstanding members of the Gálvez clan, impressive and well made, although badly preserved, and the tomb which holds the remains of the Marquis of Sonora, the all-powerful universal Minister of the Indies of Carlos III, Don José de Gálvez, who in life took care to restore and beautify the temple, as well as to build the crypt for the family pantheon.

Two centuries have mouldered over this nave and —although on Sundays the priest from the neighboring town celebrates Mass— there floats in the air a painful sense of abandon. The sacristy is in danger of ruin from leaks in the roof. There are leaks in the baptistry, too; the font in which Bernardo and his uncles were baptized is filled with rubble, and the crypt is in equally bad condition. Appeals must be made to those responsible, national or provincial authorities, organizations, entities, anonymous or public philanthropists, to come to the rescue of these walls before they are irreparably eroded by rain and forgetfulness. At least, so that the travellers and tourists who from now on, after the great effect of the Bicentennial, come to this place, following the traces of Bernardo de Gálvez, may not confirm here the inveterate and disdainful attitude of the Spaniards towards their own history.

And something more can be done. It certainly would be neither difficult nor expensive to fix up one of the typical old houses of Macharavialla as a Gálvez Museum, and bring together there portraits, canvases, engravings, uniforms, arms, escutcheons, books, charts, furnishings and mementos associated with episodes in the life of the Gálvez family in a suggestive evocation of a period —the second half of the 18th century— and of events in which they took an active part. The present moment is suitable for a proposal of this kind, given the fact that the Bicentennial celebrations are still recent, and it should be possible to collect for the hypothetical Museum pieces, statues, paintings, engravings, etc., brought together for the Spanish participation in these acts, so that these universal Malaguenians might once again be present in their own setting in Macharavialla, lengthening the traces of their lives. This presence would be complete with the placing of a simple statue of the Marquis of Sonora —the great founder of the Gálvez dynasty— in the plaza before the church as an homage to the man who always kept in his heart the image of this village which he left as a boy, with his bundle over his shoulder, in search of his fortune, managing to raise his kinsmen to the highest places in the history of their time.

Nor would it seem excessive that in the capital an expressive monument, a bare monolith, a simple plaque, should honor the memory of the Gálvez family, the most illustrious sons of Málaga in the 18th century. To José, the Minister, the city owes the founding of the Royal College of San Telmo (a branch of the Mareantes University of Sevilla), for orphan children «*who may serve in the Royal Navy and in the Indies*», setting aside for its maintenance a percentage per ton of ships which returned from America; they can also be grateful to him for the creation of the Harvesters' Loan Bank of Málaga, with an assignation of 600,000 reales in capital and a loan of two million reales, and, finally, the construction of an aqueduct (always the old, basic problem of water supply) to bring to public fountains the waters of the Guadalmedina River. Very possibly, he decided the concession to the Metropolitan Council of the «*arbitrio sobre el fruto*» which paid for the termination of the Cathedral. For his part, Miguel was the perpetual Alderman of the city; Matías and Bernardo, after all, both Viceroys, were a living testimony to Málaga in New Spain. A monument to them in the streets, in the gardens of the Park, or in Gibralfaro, might be the best way to teach the people to value and become accustomed to the sound of names today unknown in their own land.

The Gálvez family never forgot their birthplace. This is obvious in their wills and testaments. Bernardo himself, shortly before dying in Mexico, declared in his last Will: «*that there be done with the altar in Macharavialla that which has been agreed with my uncles*». For his part, the influential José, in addition to building schools, built in the town a playing-card factory in which two hundred people worker, bringing specialized craftsmen and artists from Italy and France to start the operation, to which he awarded the monopoly for the export of cards to America. Until just a short time ago there was preserved on the façade of the big house, carved in stone, a golden horse as the shield of the factory. These and other protections given to Macharavialla at that time brought it a visible prosperity such that it became known, ironically, as «*little Madrid*».

Don José de Gálvez recommended, also, that all the children of the town who had received primary education should be sent to the Court to pursue higher studies or sent to the Indies, and it is told how on one trip which the Minister made to his birthplace he astonished the people with these words: «*While I live I wish all the field labor of this town to be done by outsiders, as I propose that all the natives be men with a career, of position and, above all, educated. As long as there is a single coin in my chests I will dedicate it to that purpose*».

Such was the passion of the Gálvez for their place of birth. From here there came poor gentlemen, fallen on bad times, but with strong wings, like hawks, to undertake the flight that would carry them to posts of fortune after performing outstanding services. And to here they returned, to the luminous corner they had never forgotten, to take their places in the family pantheon in the «*Escorial of the Gálvez*».

ROOTS AND BRANCHES

The status and nobility of blood of the Gálvez of Macharavialla are demostrated in the documents set forth by the King of Arms, Don Ramón Zaro y Ortega: «*the said gentlemen, Don Mathias, Don Joseph, Don Miguel and Don Antonio Gálvez, Madrid, García and Cabrera, may use as their Coat-of-Arms that which is shown above on their rings, seals, hangings, tapestries, homes, portals, chapels, sepulchres, tombs, gold and silver jewelry and wherever else they may wish, bearing them in jousts, tornaments and other acts of honor permitted to knights and gentlemen of blood of these Realms, which the mentioned brothers are in every sense*».

The Vizcayan origin of the Gálvez family appears to be totally confirmed, also that they had their beginnings a stone's throw from Guernica. Thus, on their coat-of-arms are seen, on a silver field, the two wolves at the foot of the oak symbolic of Vizcaya, an emblem common to so many Vizcayan escutcheons.

Through out the Medieval centuries, the old chronicles mention the name of Gálvez in the most outstanding events of the Reconquest. Thus, in the legendary Battle of Clavijo, in which they added to their shield the scallop shells of St. James, and, centuries later, in the taking of Baeza, Córdoba and Sevilla with the army of Fernando III el Santo. Previously, old documents point to their presence at the siege of the Castle of Madrid, with the host of Segovia, distinguishing themselves in the fighting at Puertacerrada.

In 1240 the Gálvez won reknown in the assault on the Andalusian town of Santaella, where some of them penetrated by a postern gate in the walls of the fortress and were know ever after as the «*Gálvez of the postern*». This branch of the family remained in this Cordoban town. Notable members of the line appear, also, in Aragón and Catalonia.

However, it was to be Antón de Gálvez who would be the root and trunk of this lineage. His existence is proven by documents, as well as the brilliant services he performed for the Catholic Monarchs in the battle and surrender of Granada (1492), being rewarded for his brave conduct with dispensations and privileges, such as that of having the right to a burial spot and a fixed place for himself and those who succeded him in the parish church wherever they might live.

His descendants, noble gentlemen, settled in different parts of Andalusia, and one of them, Alonso de Gálvez, known as «*El Bermejo*», or «*El Rubio*», served in the War of the Alpujarras of Granada under the command of the Marquis of the Vélez against the bloody rebellion of the Moors of Aben-Humeya, receiving as a reward for his deeds various lands and farm settlements in Macharavialla and Benaque, where he established himself, and the civil possession of which he received from the Administrator of the Royal Treasury on January 21, 1572, hastening to place in the parish church of Macharavialla *a pew and a plaque with his arms, marking what would henceforth be the private pew of the family, in virtue of the dispensation of the Catholic Monarchs to his great-grandfather Antón de Gálvez*, as is documented by Don Isidoro Vázquez del Postigo, Marquis García del Postigo, in his solid work *History of the House of Gálvez and its Alliances*.

Without interruption the family line came down to Alonso de Gálvez, already listed as a knight, in Vélez-Málaga, in the course of the 18th century, married to Doña Ana Gallardo y Cabrera. From this marriage there were born the famous Gálvez: Matías (father of Bernardo), José, Miguel and Antonio, all born in Macharavialla, all of them called in an unforeseeable way to high position precisely when, with the premature death of their father, the family patrimony was weak, verging on poverty, the future presented itself to the four brothers as dark and hopeless.

The winds of destiny shifted, however, when Bishop Don Diego González Toro, in a pastoral visit to Macharavialla, took note of the gifts of José, an eight year old orphan at the time, acolyte of the town, and admiring the intelligence of the child, resolved to send him to the seminary in Málaga. The Bishop died soon after, but his successor on the diocese, Don Gaspar de Molina, gave him similar protection. The prelate, however, aware of the lack of religious vocation in the boy, sent him to Salamanca, recommending his entrance in the University. There he studied Law, continuing his education at the University of Alcalá de Henares.

THE LAW BEFORE THE KING

Thus began a meteoric career. Famous attorney of the City and the Court, friend of the intellectuals of his time, he became the private secretary of the Marquis of Grimaldi, Prime Minister of Carlos III. It is told how he brilliantly won a famous case defending an important foreign firm against the State. His prestige grew and the King, in an audience with the young jurist, asked how he had dared to defend a case against the Crown. *«Sire, before the King there is the law»*, answered Gálvez in a case which became historic. He made such a good impression on the Monarch that a little later he named him official attorney for HRH Prince Don Carlos and Mayor of the Household and Court, a position which brought him into close contact with the Count of Aranda an other influential politicians, such as the famous Campomanes and Floridablanca, who were to favor him so strongly.

In February of 1765 he is named Visitor General of New Spain and a month later he is designated as a member of the Council of the Indies. Invested with great authority, even as regards the Viceroy, whose actions he was to fiscalize, Gálvez arrives in Mexico on his first official mission. He acted energetically, unmasked corruption and abuse and took an active part in the expulsion of the Jesuits from New Spain, repressing hardly the threatening riots caused by this measure, revealing the existence of a deep plot which used the exile of the priests as an excuse. While the Viceroy, in an unique decree, advised «*the vassals of the great monarch who occupies the throne of Spain that they were born to be quiet and obey and not to discuss and form opinions on Governmental affairs*», Gálvez placed himself at the head of the troops and hung ninety of the mutineers. The Company of Jesus had 678 priests in Mexico and only fifteen were excused from exile due to physical impediments. On April 13th the Jesuits embarked in Veracruz. They left abandoned the missions they had looked after: 17 in Tarahumera, 29 in Sonora and 15 in California. To replace them, Gálvez called the Franciscans to Mexico.

Gálvez decided to undertake the pacification of the province of Sonora and the task of populating California and, after naming Don Carlos Francisco de Croix as new Viceroy, put himself at the head of a great expedition, «*the greatest ever seen in Mexico since Hernán Cortés*», financed by popular subscription, without calling on the public Treasury. To transport the troops by sea, Gálvez had built in San Blas two barkentines, the «*San Carlos*» and the «*Príncipe*». Establishing his headquarters in Santa Ana, he promoted the Franciscan missions on the coat and called to his side the heroic Fray Junípero Serra,

«*Evangelist of the Pacific Ocean*», offering him «*abundant soup and tight lodgings*», outlining, hand in hand with him, in an efficient and mutually understood team, the plan for foundations in San Diego, in Monterrey and in San Buenaventura. Father Francisco Palau, the stupendous chronicler and companion of the Mallorcan monk, transcribes the impressive dialogue in which Fray Junípero, man of God, asks the Visitor of the Indies, man of State:

«*Sir, and why does San Francisco have no mission?*»

«*If San Francisco wants a mission, have him let us discover a good harbor and we will put one there under his advocacy*».

And, in effect, not much later there was rediscovered the harbor which had been explored by Sebastián Vizcaíno in 1602, and so there was the Mission of San Francisco, the cell from which grew the great city of today. It was in 1769 when the expedition of Captain Gaspar de Portolá, Governor of California, which had sailed from San Diego, sighted the bay. The definitive founding of San Francisco was made by Juan Bautista de Anza, in 1776, precisely the same year as the Declaration of Independence in Philadelphia.

The effigy of the tireless Franciscan, who travelled more than eleven thousand kilometers in setting up his foundations, may be seen in the Californian plaza of Ventura; at its foot may be read this inscription: «*Fray Junípero Serra, 1713-1784. The civilization of California began with the foundation of the first nine missions*».

Gálvez based himself on the missionairies to create, with clear political vision, advanced centers of population and civilization in those distant regions, in which the Indians could be instructed in schools and farmt, learn skills and crafts and settle down into a hard-working, peaceful life. Parallel to this he posted garrisons and military detachments to defend the towns and insure communications. These enclaves of progress grew repidly under the stimulous and guidance of the missionaries and there was an influx of emigrants and settlers. In a short time, thousands of Indians were converted to the Christian faith and 21 churches were built. In the first foundations the missionary said Mass under an improvised shelter and cried: *Hear, pagans, come to the holy church; come and receive the faith of Jesus Christ».* When Fray Junípero celebrated his first Mass on Californian soil there stepped forth an Indian who followed the liturgy with close attention. He was the first to be baptized in the province.

The chronicles of those days tell us that the Indian women —mothers— offered to nurse the Child Jesus whose image was over the altar. Little by little the Indians were taught to work, and they soon came to look for and recognize in those crossed sticks and the bell over the missions, a school of peace and human assistance.

Only twenty years after the arrival of the Spaniards in California, in a territory previously desolate and hostile, there were 8,000 persons, without counting the children; 6,000 horses; 27,000 cows; 22,000 sheep and a greater number of hogs, domestic fowls, etc. In a single harvest there were reaped 37,000 bushels of grain. The «*San*

Carlos» has been called the *«Mayflower of the West»*, as it landed in 1769, in San Diego, a few head of cattle from Castilla, which were the foundation for the great California herd.

On the other hand, this rosary of missions in Upper California had an evident historic repercussion, as with the colonization of these regions, Spain guaranteed the independence of the American Pacific coast, not from the English, but from the Russians who, after 1764, planned to expand along this edge of the continent, coming from Arcángel and Kamchatka, as Czar Paul had founded the *«Imperial Russo-American Company»* for the fur trade. After the initial expedition of the Dane Behring and the Russian Tschrikoff, there were a number of other, one under the command of Captain Karanitzin. The instructions of Don José de Gálvez to the pilot Juan Pérez, the first explorer of the coasts of Alaska (followed later by many Spanish navigators, among them Lieutenant Juan Francisco de la Bodega), are sufficiemtly clear and expressive: *«You must consider, in the first place, this expedition is undertaken to and aimed at establishing the Catholic religion, extend the domination of the King and protect this Peninsula from the ambitious moves of a foreign nation».*

Faced with this threat, well-understood by the government in Madrid, as it had been alerted by the Spanish ambassador in St. Petersburg, it was essential to take possession of these territories, populate them make possible their defense, closing the way to the Russians. This was the reason that Gálvez, following instructions from the

Court, backed the spread to the North of Fray Junípero Serra's missions, escorted by military detachments.

In this way, then, Spain served the cause of American independence in the Pacific, as it did in the East cooperating in the liberation of the colonies of the Atlantic coast, although faced with different antagonists, Russians on the one side and British on the other. As is logical, acting in this way Spain was looking after its own territories, but it must be recognized that this convenience corresponded completely with the interests of the colonists. By saving the Pacific region from the appetites of the Czar, the government in Madrid made an outstanding contribution to the future United States.

In the remains of the old Spanish Missions are buried the roots of the people of California as an historic community. One day among the fathers and founders of the United States, together with Washington, Jefferson, etc., will be included those others who founded States in the Union: Junípero Serra, Ponce de León, Hernando de Soto, Alvar Núñez Cabeza de Vaca, Oñate, Vázquez Coronado... The same idea is seen in the words of President John F. Kennedy: «*Too many Americans think America was discovered in 1620, when the Pilgrim Fathers came to my own State, and forget the tremendous adventure of the 16th century and the beginnings of the 17th in the South and Southwest of the United States*». For his part, the great student of Spain, Charles F. Lummis, puts it this way: «*If Spain had not existed four hundred years ago, the United States would not exist today*».

Meanwhile, Don Antonio María Bucareli y Ursúa, Master

of the Order of St. John, had succeded the Marquis de Croix as Viceroy of New Spain. On sending him the despatches naming him, Marshal O'Reilly, from the Court, wrote to Bucareli: *«I think it convenient to tell you that you should listen to whatever Gálvez may want to tell you, without his ever knowing or inferring what you may think».* The answer from the wise Bucareli shows clear praise for the Visitor: *«We have not had the slightest difficulty and you know that I am not a man who agrees to everything; such is his care and understanding».*

Suffering from a strange mental illness, never clarified, and which has caused various interpretations, José de Gálvez had to interrupt his work. His health recovered, he returns to Spain in 1772 and the King awards him the Order of Carlos III. His direct experience of the American reality, lived on the spot during this journey, the detailed knowledge he came to have of the Indian problems, had a positive influence on the new structure of the Viceroyalties and on a series daring reforms he was to promote from the Council of the Indies. Thus, in 1776, he put into effect a new organization of New Spain, creating the so-called Interior Provinces (New Vizcaya, Sinaloa, Sonora, Coahuila, the two Californias, New Mexico and Texas) as an entity segregated from the Viceroy of Mexico, whose General Command was established in Chihuahua *«with the very important aim»* —they are his words, suited to a man with true political vision— *«of giving spirit and movement to such vast territories, naturally rich, which in a few years may form an empire equal to or greater than this in Mexico».*

In 1776, Carlos III names Gálvez Secretary of State in the Office of the Indies. From then, until his death, he developed a tireless activity as a legislator, reflected in innumerable acts of government with ambitious aims. The first reform he put into practice, and in which he collaborated with the Count of Floridablanca, was that of free trade between the Peninsula and the Overseas Provinces. Gálvez, by Decree of October 12, 1778, abolished the trade monopoly of galleons and fleets and opened thirty-three ports to free trade, which caused a great increase in commercial traffic and quadrupled the income from customs duties, increasing as well tre value of exports. Industry in Catalonia increased notably, as well as naval construction in various ports and the organization of circular voyages between Spain and America. In 1785 he promoted the new foundation of the Royal Philipines Company, with a capital of eight million pesos, reserving three thousand shares for the inhabitants of Manila, «*because*» —says the Royal text— «*the prosperity of the Philipine Islands and its inhabitants has been the principal motive behind my paternal desire to protect and distribute this enterprise, and I have wished that in addition to the advantages they will enjoy thanks to the improvement in agriculture, industry and naval affairs, they may have a direct share in the earnings of this Company*». The Company lasted until 1834.

Another initiative of the Minister was the establishment of the Intendencies in America, replacing the old Mayoralities. The Intendents of the Indies had responsibilities similar to those of the present Civil Governors and contributed to a greater fluidity in the administration of the Viceroyalties. Later measures affected the establishment of tobacco rents, reforms in the slave trade and, ahead of its time in a social sense, the creation of credit institutions for farm-workers and craftsmen. In the hall of the Economic Society of Friends of the Country, in Málaga, is preserved an allegoric painting, by Insa, in which is shown the Malaguenian people, headed by Don José and Don Miguel de Gálvez —«*beloved members of the chapter and zealous patricians*»— before Carlos III, in 1776, showing their gratitude for the approval of the Credit Bank for Harvest-workers.

On the cultural plane one must attribute to Don José de Gálvez the founding of the Archive of the Indies at the suggestion of Don Juan Bautista Muñoz, famed scientist and man of learning, Chief Cosmographer of the Indies. In 1778 Gálvez arranged that the fundamental American documents in the Archive of Simancas and in other ministerial departments, convents, etc., should be brought together in a specialized collection of books, maps and writings on Indian affairs, a splendid initiative which he carried out, installing the new Archive —universally used today in the world of the investigators— in the Casa Lonja in Sevilla. The Minister had an excellent private collection of minerals and plants which he constantly increased, having them send valuable and exotic pieces from the farthest provinces of the Empire. Gálvez concei- ved the idea of making navigable the Bravo, or Río Grande del Norte, which running from New Mexico through the provinces of New Vizcaya and Coahuila to empty into the Gulf would have made a great commercial route, as was the Mississippi. He even encouraged the initiative of Mr. de la Fer to join the two oceans, the Atlantic and the Pacific, by a canal across the Isthmus of Panama, the first antecedent of what exists today.

In 1785 he was rewarded by the King with the title of Marquis of Sonora. The intelligent man of finances, Cabarrús, said of him: «... *Gálvez, not completely appreciated by his contemporaries, but who, in the midst of many mistakes, is the only Minister I have dealt with who could be moved to enthusiasm for the good and glory of his country and who only lacked to be a great man to have been born forty years later*».

He chose for his final resting place a corner of the humble crypt of the church in Macharavialla beneath the altar on which, as a child, he had so often assisted in the celebration of the Mass, near the cliffs up which he had climbed with his flock to the highest point of the summit, from which can be seen the sea of Málaga.

Don José de Gálvez is, without doubt, one of the notable statesmen of our 18th century. A politician of open character and practical and realistic criteria, faithful to the spirit of «*illustration*», he attempted to reform and bring up to date the heavy and creaking machinery of the Empire. Skillful and resolute, he hastened to create sources of wealth, production and commerce, mobilizing the energies of the country. Other ministers of the period may have surpassed him in the formulation of a State philosophy or in the algebra of foreign politic, none in knowledge of the instrumentalization of the techniques of government, nor in knowledge of the problems and needs of his time and in the adoption of adequate solutions. His great ambition was the social progress and development of Spain, its economic and cultural flourishing and, above all, the efficient administration of the State. His personal ambition, possibly, was the elevation of de Gálvez family, as he believ his brothers to possess talents and aptitudes which should be used; he managed to raise them with his backing and unlimited help, and they did not deceive him. On the contrary, they contributed, through multiple services, to sustain and increase his power.

Universal minister of a great King, his figure truly recalls that of another Joseph, the prudent son of the patriarch Jacob, to whom the Pharoah, as the Bible tells us, delivered the government of Egypt. Both held power because of their merits and not through royal favoritism; both called on their brothers. Such is the theme of a bit of doggerel of the time, one of the many which his infinite number of enemies dedicated to the omnipotent Marquis of Sonora.

THE DECK WITH THE FIVE KINGS

Among the Gálvez brothers, Miguel also studied Law in Salamanca and Alcalá de Henares. Perpetual Alderman of Málaga, he carried out efficient diplomatic missions, such as that which took him to Prussia as Minister Plenipotentiary, being well received by Frederick the Great. Destined later to St. Petersburg, he carried out a positive activity, serving as mediator in the war between Russia and Sweden. A good advertiser of the wines of his land, he wrote to the Governing Board of the Brotherhood of Wine-makers in Málaga asking them to send a selected lot of their wines to the Empress Catherine of Russia, who, after tasting the delights of the «Málaga», removed the duties in the ports of the vast country for such an excellent product.

He reported exactly as to the Russian pretensions towards the western coasts of North America, a burning subject for Spain because of our interests in Upper California. Without doubt these reports were especially valuable to his brother José in relation with the establishing of the Franciscan missions on that coast. The embassy of Miguel de Gálvez was short and he died during his return to Madrid in the city of Gotha. His last wish was that he should be buried in the family pantheon in Macharavialla.

As to Antonio, the youngest of the brothers, there are few reports. He was entrusted with high positions, such as the Commanding General of the Customs of the Bay of Cádiz. He reached the grade of Field Marshal. He was the protagonist of a peculiar episode which took place in Morocco. When he was bound for Cuba in command of a Catalonian ship he was taken prisoner by the Moroccan corsair Alí Péres and taken to the port of Salé. From there Don Antonio de Gálvez wrote to the Sultan of Morocco, Sidi Mohamed: «*I beg of Your Royal Majesty that you issue your Royal Decree so that the ship may be set free and continue its journey; and that I, who have had the pleasure of coming to Your Majesty's domains, with your Royal permission, will come in person to kiss you Royal feet and take your Royal desires, should they be given, to the King, my lord, whom may God keep, and with the assistance of my brother the Minister deal with the peace and concord which he so much desires for all the subjects of both Crowns, which I will do without fail in everything Your Royal Majesty may wish to command me*».

Having received the letter, the Sultan ordered a reprimand for Alí Péres and wrote to Don Antonio authorizing him to visit him. The Moroccan courtiers believed they were dealing with an emissary of Carlos III come to make peace. This alarmed, above all, a Spanish Franciscan, Fray José de Boltas, a resident there and well acquainted with the relations between Spain and Morocco, in which he acted as mediator, who feared that all might be undone by the intervention of Don Antonio. At last, Gálvez and Boltas had an interview with Sidi Mohamed with satisfactory results, the Sultan sending a series of letters and presents to Carlos III and Floridablanca, which opened the way for peace negotiations.

The marriage of Don Antonio de Gálvez and Doña Mariana Ramírez de Velasco being childless, they adopted a daughter born in Málaga, in 1768, whom many supposed to be the bastard daughter of Carlos III because of these words which appear in the will of her adopted parents: «... *whom we have raised and educated from infancy in our home and have given and give her the treatment of daughter, because we state that she is of illustrious and distinguished parents whose names we do not set down for just reasons which prevent it...*».

Doña María Rosa de Gálvez, which was her name, had literary pretensions and a stormy biography. Married to Captain Don José Cabrera, she abandoned the conjugal roof and moved to that of the Prince of the Peace, Don Manuel Godoy y Alvarez de Farias, with whom she maintained erotic-poetic relations and she dedicated her ode «*The Campaingn on Portugal*» to the detested strong man of Carlos IV, to whom she gave a poem every morning at breakfast; a stiff test, and at such a time of day, nor do we know how Don Manuel took it. She premiered a number of pieces in the theaters of Madrid, along the line of those of Bretón de los Herreros, and died about 1807.

There still remains Matías, the first-born. He was born, like his parents and brothers, in Macharavialla, in 1717, and goes down in history not only as the father of Bernardo de Gálvez, but for his own well-balanced personality and achievements. He went into the Army, reviving the military vocation of the Gálvez family in other centuries. His intelligence and character, and also the patronage of his brother José, as was said by the family's implacable enemies, raised him from Ensign to Captain General. His first commands were in the Canary Islands, where he was Governor of the Paso Alto Castle in Tenerife and second General-in-Command of the Archipelago.

In 1778 he was named Captain General and President of the Royal Audience of Guatemala. With the declaration of war between Spain and Great Britain, he had an outstanding intervention at the head of his troops in the surrender of San Fernando de Omoa Castle, which some time before had been taken by the English, capturing important booty. On receiving congratulations, Matías de Gálvez replied: *«I, gentlemen, did not come to retake Omoa, but to die on the field»*. He later mounted a victorious expedition against Roatán Island and drove the enemy from the establishments of Quepriva, Ministrie and Siniboya. At the defense of a coastal fort in Nicaragua, a girl conducted herself with bravery, the daughter of the artillery Captain José Herrera who commanded the position, Rafaela. With her father dead, as well as most of the defenders in the English attack, Rafaela took his place and fired the cannons with such good fortune that, one of their ships being struck, the British raised the siege. Carlos III, on the recommendation of Gálvez, rewarded his improvised «*artillery-man*», with a life pension. In 1958, the President of the Republic of Guatemala, Idígoras, ordered that the port and naval district of Santo Tomás de la Bahía should take the name of Matías de Gálvez in memory of these actions.

Let us stop for a moment for this short parenthet his. Around the year 1780, the Gálvez brothers, simultaneously, although in different settings, in different fields, were at the zenith of their glory. Matías, as we have seen, had just obtained definitive successes in Guatemala, Nicaragua and Honduras which cause him to be named nothing less than Viceroy of New Spain. Miguel is a robed Minister of the Council of War, President of the Royal Academy of Law, Mayor of the Household and Court, Governor, Superintendent, member of an infinity of Boards and Councils and has the road open to his brilliant embassies in Europe. For his part, Antonio has reached the rank of Field Marshal, the highest in the Army. And, above all others, José. José at the peak of the government, but in discreet shadow, close to His Majesty, managing the threads and pieces on the fluid table of politics, where what is difficult is not to arrive, but to remain.

Matías, José, Miguel and Antonio. Four impoverished gentlemen with necessity nipping at their heels. They were at the point of sinking forever into the fields of their land, hoeing the vineyards and herding goats along the mountain trails. But now they have reached the top. Now they are like the four Kings —gold, cups, swords and clubs— in the Spanish deck of cards, those cards which were printed precisely in the family seat of the Gálvez, below the church, in the «*industrial zone*» of the village, in that factory above whose entrance gallops in stone a golden horse. Four Kings, each one printed in bright colors. And there still remains another card, another King, that of the triumph, the card of Bernardo de Gálvez, winner of all the tricks in the game of war, staking heavily against the English in a life and death game which will end with him driving them from the Gulf of Mexico. Five Kings, not four, in the decks of cards from Macharavialla.

At this time, when Bernardo was Captain General of Cuba and Matías Viceroy of New Spain, there appeared on the walls of Mexico this lampoon summing up the increasing influence of the Gálvez:

> «*Who rules in this world?*
> *José, the first;*
> *Matías, the second,*
> *And Bernardo, the third.*
>
> *Fiscal... viceroy,*
> *Viceroy... minister,*
> *And Minister... King.*
>
> *The father here,*
> *the son, in Havana*
> *and the Spirit in Spain*».

Let us go on. Named Viceroy of New Spain, Matías de Gálvez made a triumphal entry into Mexico in 1783. His governmental activity was brilliant and prosperous to the extreme. He developed the cultural institutions, created the first Mexican newspaper —«*La Gaceta de México*»— the School of Drawing, the Bank of San Carlos, notably beautified the capital, set out to rebuild Chapultepec Palace, the place of recreation of the Aztec rulers. He stood out, above all, for his excellent character modesty and sympathy, which made his memory imperishable among the Mexican. Innumerable anecdotes remain of his simplicity and frankness. Thus, while inspecting with his entourage the paving of Calle de la Palma he saw a man wearing cured buckskin hides. The Viceroy called him and spoke to him at length as to the methods of curing hides and said to his companio like a simple Andalusian farmer: «*Gentlemen, they are much better than those I wore when I worked my fields*».

«*He is gifted*» —said on August 9, 1785, Don Eusebio Ventura Beleña, Judge commisioned to report on the conduct, government and abilities of Don Matías de Gálvez— «*virtue, moderation and affability with all persons and especially with the poor and miserable, to which is added his love of justice, which is joined to an admirable prudence in matters of peace and mercy, being at the same time highly honest and disinterested, aware and active in benefit of the public good, which accumulation of unique qualities have made him win the hearts of all. In proof of which I cite two cases in which his generous mercy may be seen*». The first of these cases is one in which

39

one person claimed from another the payment of four thousand pesos he had loaned him, without success, and recurring to the Viceroy, he called the who parties together and, proven the truth of the facts, called on the creditor to concede a new period to the debtor, and as this was not possible because of his urgent need of the money, he went into his own Chamber and brought four thousand pesos in gold which he gave to the claimant, telling the debtor that now it was to him, the Viceroy, to whom he owed them, paying them when he was able.

A good portrait of Matías de Gálvez hangs in one of the halls of the Gálvez Palace in Málaga, present residence of Doña Josefina de Gálvez, widow of the heroic Captain Carlos Haya, and daughter of a famous physician of Málaga, Dr. Gálvez. The painting, in gentle tones, reflects the calm charm of the man. In his hands he holds a letter to his son congratulating him on his triumphs, and whose lines we can read: «*Dear Bernardo, the joy of your conquests you owe to God, and your advancements to the King; be, then, grateful to both these Majesties to count on the blessing of your loving father: Matías de Gálvez*», words almost hidden in the painting, but which give it an intense vibrancy, making us feel the invisible presence of the person to whom the letter is directed and inviting us to learn more about him.

THE HOUR OF BERNARDO DE GALVEZ

One day in 1776 there arrives in New Orleans, capital of Louisiana, a Spanish officer. He immediately presented himself to the Governor, Don Luis de Unzaga, together with his letters of commission which are signed by the Captain General of Carlos III, Don Alejandro O'Reilly, and whose text, in military terms, says: «*Lieutenant-Colonel Don Bernardo de Gálvez, Captain of Grenadiers in the Infantry Regiment of Sevilla, has been named by the King as chief of the battalion stationed in this city of New Orleans*». At the foot of the letter there is a personal post-script from O'Reilly: «*The above has instructions and will present them at once. He is a person of the highest esteem and his uncle, the Minister of the Indies, is a very particular friend. I will be grateful for any attention you may show him*».

The young officer was exactly 30 years old, as he came into this world in Macharavialla on July 25, 1746, son of Matías de Gálvez and of Doña María Josefa de Madrid Gallardo. The day of his birth King Felipe V died in the El Pardo Palace. On this occasion the funeral dirges blended in the streets with the military marches announcing the victories of the Spanish arms in Milan. The star of the new-born, as is noted by his biographer and countryman, Sebastián Souvirón, twinkled to heroic music.

And, in effect, following the paternal example, Bernardo chose the military profession. Cadet in the Academy in Avila, at 16 he enlisted as a volunteer in the war with Portugal, in which he fought as an infantry Lieutenant.

In 1765 he embarked for New Spain in the army of General Don Juan de Villalba. In Mexico he coincided with his uncle, Don José, who as Royal Visitor was traveling in the Viceroyalty. Captain in Chihuahua in the expedition of Don Lope de Cuéllar, he was soon named to replace him. Gálvez was 24 years old and Commanding General of New Vizcaya and Sonora. He fought the Opatas Indians and made an effective alliance with them. The Opatas obligated themselves to fight the unfriendly Indian nations and named as their Chief Gálvez himself.

His first outstanding military campaingn was against the much-feared Apache Indians who with their ferocity and attacks were spreadind destruction through all the regions of the North, raising a sombre obstacle to their colonization. Bernardo commanded a troop of 200 men who in their march through inhospitable deserts had to support great hurricanes and floods. Their food supplies spoiled by the water, hungry and demoralized, they reached the Pecos River in Texas without having found the enemy. When the men spoke of returning to Chihuahua and giving up the effort, Gálvez addressed them in the classic manner of military oratory with these words which seemed to recall those of Cortes, according to Porras:

«Companions: The day has come to make the final effort... To return to Chihuahua with the shame of having wasted time and money and having achieved nothing is not for men of honor. I will go on alone if there is none to follow me. I will bring a scalp back to Chihuahua or I will pay with my life for the King's bread I have eaten; go back those of faint heart and follow me those who wish to share my hardships». He spurred his horse and crossed the river. All the troopers followed him swearing «that they would follow him to the death, that they would eaten their horses and then stone and that they would never abandon him».

Before dawn they came across the Apache camp and without waiting for day to break, with a shout of «Santiago!», they charged the Indians. «28 Indians met death that morning and 36 were captured. The booty included 204 animals and more than 2,000 pesos in deer and buffalo hides. Relieving their hunger with the food taken from the enemy, the return to Chihuahua was begun». A few days later, however, the teams and caravans of the Mexican mule-drivers who supplied Chihuahua were attacked. The Indians carried off a thousand animals, loads of silver and muskets and killed seven men. The attacks of the warriors from their nomad camps were incessant on the herda of horses and mules of the strong-points, for which it was necessary to reinforce the garrisons.

Six months later Gálvez led another campaign in which he used as guides the prisoners taken in the previous action. It was the first time the Apaches were agreeable to accept the guidance of a white man. The war became endless in these unpopulated areas, the strokes and counterstrokes of the Indians multiplied as, consummate horsemen, they had managed to domesticate the horses escaped into the mountains Gálvez was wounded on several occasions; on the last of them he was carried off with two spear wounds in the chest and an arrow in his left arm. The struggle was to go on for year after year along the whole border, maintaining the forts and foundations with great sacrifices until, at last, a stable peace could be made with the Apaches.

These campaigns in the province of Sonora allowed Gálvez to experience and come to know in detail a specific type of warfare: that practiced by the Indian nations. This experience was going to prove extraordinarily useful in the actions he would have to face in the Mississippi Valley fighting powerful tribes allied with the English. It allowed him, also, to know the character, the customs and the laws of the Indian people, and through this knowledge win the friendship of their warriors and chiefs, and establish lasting treaties and pacts with them. There are still preserved, written or painted on deer-skin or on the skins of the great fish of the Mississippi, copies of agreements and alliances drawn up by the mediation of Gálvez during his Governorship of Louisiana between His Catholic Majesty of Spain and the great Indian chiefs, setting limits, frontiers and peace conditions, copies of which some tribes still preserve in the melancholy of their reservations, as a testimony and historic reinvindication of the sovereignty and rights of the Indian communities over their ancient territories usurped by the American colonists.

Gálvez even left behind a work entitled: «Notes and reflexions on the war fought in America by the Spanish troops against the Apaches and other barbarous nations», in which he tells of his experiences in these campaigns and makes unique observations, such as his recommendation that the Indians should use firearms rather than arrows and spears as they would be limited by the problem of supplies of ammunition.

In 1771 Bernardo returned to Spain accompanying his uncle, the Visitor, who was also returning to the Peninsula and who asked and received this favor from the Viceroy Bucareli. He was replaced as military commander in Sonora by Don Hugo O'Connor, recommended by and a relative of General O'Reilly, both of Irish origin. Before embarking, Bernardo left behind in Veracruz, as students in the College of San Gregorio, fourteen Apache prisoners; war, for Gálvez, did not mean the extermination of the conquered.

Once at Court, he asked and received permission to leave active service and went to France to undertake studies in the perfection of military science, with the consequent learning of the language, which had great importance to his future and popularity in Louisiana, as this province was French in culture and the population, as is logical, was magnificently impressed when Gálvez was named Governor and they found he could speak to them in their own language.

In 1775, Gálvez is once again in Spain and is Captain of the Infantry Regiment of Sevilla. With this unit, and under the supreme command of Marshal O'Reilly, he took part in the landing and assault on the fortress of Algiers, where his conduct was heroic, as gravely wounded he refused to be carried from the field. Only when the white banner with the fleur-de-lys of the Bourbons waved over the fortress of Algiers did he allow his soldiers to evacuate him.

Gálvez was promoted to Lieutenant-Colonel for merits of war and, after convalescence, destined to the Military Academy in Avila, which he had left years before as a Cadet. Now Gálvez was returning to the quiet of the walled Castilian city and ready to educate other aspirants in the art of war, giving them the benefit of his own experiences, when he was called to the Court. Marshal O'Reilly tells him that His Majesty, at the proposal of the Royal Council, had named him head of the Fixed Garrison Regiment in New Orleans to «*carry out my service, provide for the defense and develop the population and commerce of the province of Louisiana and to have in that important place a person of my complete confidence*».

The nomination, then, was not only military, but political as well and made it evident that within a short time Bernardo would take over the Governorship, as the forty years of service in the Indies of the veteran and competent Unzaga called for his relief and substitution by a young and competent man, capable of identifying with the problems, responsibilities and interests of a vast province boiling over because of its strategic location and its proximity to the American colonies risen in war against Great Britain.

And so it happened. Months after his arrival in New Orleans, he took over as Acting Governor from Don Luis de Unzaga, who retired at his own request. The hour of Bernardo de Gálvez had struck.

LOUISIANA ON THE DIPLOMATIC
CHESS-BOARD

The province of Louisiana (named in honor of Louis XIV), ceded by France to Spain in 1763, at the end of the Seven Year's War, in compensation for the loss of Florida, was an immense territory with the Mississippi and its tributaries as its spinal column, which extended from the mouth of the River of the Palisades (the name given by the Spanish explorerers who discovered it in the 16th century because of the enormous number of tree trunks carried down by its waters) to the region of the Great Lakes on the border with Canada. Its frontiers were marked by the forts of New Orleans, Santa Genoveva, St. Louis and Fort Arkansas and followed the left banks of the Mississippi and Missouri to Kansas and the Red River to Cadadacho.

Primitive Louisiana (infinitely greater in size than the present State of this name, as it included the territories of Minnesota, Wisconsin, Missouri, Illinois, Kentucky, Arkansas, Tennessee and Mississippi) had a scant population, limited to French colonists who exploited the rice, tobacco and cotton plantations and, preferably, the trade in skins. A chain of military posts along the Mississippi guaranteed the river navigation and the trade with the powerful Indian nations who lived in the great forests.

New Orleans was the heart of an insufficiently explored province, and the Mississippi, its aorta, which brought to the city the distant beat of the struggle of the colonies risen against the English; a war which was heard along the whole frontier. The posts and detachments set at the mouths of the great tributaries detected the movement of troops, the pacts and alliances of the Indian tribes and the incessant traffic of hundreds of boats (more than 400 boats went up and down the river in Spring and Fall with their cargoes of martin, beaver and fox skins). The reports of these garrisons, joined to those of the spies and couriers who moved through the region flowed into the office of the Governor of Louisiana, the man who had to make the decisions.

It was not the first time that the Spaniards had controlled the territory, as it had been discovered more than two hundred years before when Hernando de Soto and Fray Marcos de Niza, excited by the tales of Alvar Núñez Cabeza de Vaca, organized an expedition of 600 soldiers and 213 horses to explore that unknown world in a fabulous adventure. Already in 1519, Alonso Alvarez de Pineda had seen the delta of the Mississippi, and in 1528, the expedition under Pánfilo de Narváez, with whom was Cabeza de Vaca, explored one of the arms of the great river. They were the first white men who saw, astonished, the immense river «*a half league across*», which the Indians called «*Meact Massipi*», that is, «*father of waters*» and which, according to the expressive chronicle, «*if a man on the other side were still, it could not be seen if he were a man or something else*». Between 1539 and 1542 Soto covered 35,000 square miles from Tampa to North Carolina, Tennessee, Alabama and Mississippi, going as far West as Arkansas and Oklahoma, and then on to Texas, to return and descend the Mississippi to the Gulf of Mexico. On the death of Hernando de Soto, his soldiers buried their Captain in the bed of the river so that the Indians might not discover his grave.

In addition to providing defense, population and good administration for those territories, the essential mission of the new Governor of Louisiana, Bernardo de Gálvez, was to be that of translating into acts the attitude of the Spanish monarchy towards the revolution of the thirteen American colonies, according to precise instructions from the Council of the Indies of which Gálvez was the bearer. In synthesis, the attitude adopted by the government of Carlos III consisted in supporting the independence movement by all means within its capacity, but taking great care, for the moment, to avoid a «*causus belli*» with Great Britain. The objective of this policy of aid to the rebel colonists was to weaken the English position in America, and indirectly in Europe, and, if possible, eliminat its presence in the Gulf of Mexico (where England had the two Floridas, the island of Jamaica and a series of forts on the coast of Honduras), to guarantee the security of the Spanish domains in the New World and their commerce, threatened by the British preponderance.

Let us insert a paragraph to explain succintly the beginning of the arme conflict between England and its American colonies. Let us begin by naming these thirteen colonies. They were: Virginia, New York, Massachusetts, Rhode Island, Delaware, North Carolina, New Jersey, New Hampshire, Maryland, Connecticut, South Carolina, Pennsylvania and Georgia. They were born from very different roots; Virginia (thus named in honor of the daughter of Henry VIII, Elizabeth, the Virgin Queen, and Massachusetts grew from the settlements of the first English emmigrants. It was May, 1607, when three ships sent by the Virginia Company, with 105 men, raised a settlement at the mouth of the James River, which they called (in honor of King James) Jamestown; thirteen years later, in 1620, there arrived at Cape Cod the Pilgrims in the «*Mayflower*», with another hundred persons. Before landing, 41 men of the group signed the famous «*Mayflower Pact*»: «*In the name of God... we agree to join and combine together in a civil nation*». A little later there arose Plymouth (recalling the English city from which they had sailed), with John Carver as first Governor. Rhode Island was created in 1636 by Roger Williams, guaranteeing religious freedom after 1663. Pennsylvania owes its founding to the famous Quaker, William Penn; Georgia to James Oglethorpe and Maryland to a notable Catholic, Lord Baltimore. In 1664 the Dutch founded New York.

With enormous effort and persistence the colonies developed, basing themselves on agriculture —the great «*boom*» was the raising and export of tobacco, whose seeds were imported from the Spanish Antilles— and also on industry. Around 1776 the population was more than two million. As a consequence of the Seven Years War, ended in 1763, Great Britain destroyed the French power in North America, acquiring, among others, the dominions of Canada; England faced a harsh economic crisis. The land war had caused heavy expenses and the Government in London decided that these expenses should fall, in good part, on those who, theoretically, hat most benefitted from these conquests: the American colonies. To this end, they established new taxes which were energetically rejected. The first warning was the Stamp Act, a stamp which was required on every document. The colonists burned the stamps.

«*We have*» —they said— «*the same rights as the English, who cannot be taxed without their consent*». (No taxation without representation; «*we do not want taxation without representation in Parliament*»). The situation deteriorated progressively, without retreat by either side. The English adopted a position of strength: «*The North Americans must fear us before they love us*». The tea tax caused a popular outburst. When a cargo of tea arrived in Boston, the rebels threw it into the bay. In September of 1774 the representatives of the colonies met in Philadelphia to take collective decisions.

On April 19, 1775, in a country village, Lexington, in Massachusetts, the troops sent to confiscate munitions found a line of armed farmers who closed the way. There the shooting began. With this uprising the a revolution began. Two hundred British soldiers were killed or wounded. On June 17, 1775, three thousand English veterans tried to take a hill on the outskirts of Boston. They lost more than a thousand men. On June 17, 1776, Richard Henry Lee, of Virginia, said: «*These united colonies are, and by right should be, free and independent states*». On July 4, 1776, the solemn Declaration of Independence announced the birth of a new nation: «*All men are created equal, that they are endowed by their Creator with certain inalienable Rights, that among these are Life, Liberty and the pursuit of Happiness*».

The war spread throughout the country, and to lead the joint army General George Washington was called. The struggle suffered many alternatives. At the end of 1777 (and once he knew of the surrender of General Burgoyne to Gates), Louis XVI officially recognized the independence of the United States, signing a treaty of friendship with the new nation. In the middle of this same year Marquis Paul de La Fayette, who had sailed from the Guipuzcoan port of Pasajes with the «*placet*» of the Spanish authorities (the French had stopped him from sailing from Burdeos), in «*Le Victoire*», reached Philadelphia to join General Washington with an introduction from Benjamin Franklin, with whom he had become intimate in Paris. La Fayette offered to fight as a simple soldier in the army of the United States. He was attached, with the rank of General, to Washington's staff. Thanks to his efforts there sailed a French fleet under the command of Count D'Estaing, with twelve ships of the line, five frigates and four thousand marines. They achieved some successes, but no decisive results, and returned to Europe. In 1780 there sailed a second squadron under the orders of Admiral De Grasse and General Rochambeau, commanding an army of 6,000 men, defeating in Chesapeake Bay the English Admiral Graves. Finally, General Cornwallis surrendered to Washington at Yorktown. It was October 19, 1781. The war had ended.

In 1777, the French Minister of Foreign Affairs, Count Granvier de Vergennes proposed, in accordance with the spirit of the Family Pact, an offensive alliance of France and Spain with the Americans against the English. *«Providence has provided this opportunity»* —wrote Vergennes to the Spanish government— *«for the humilliation of a voracious power. The result for both Crowns will be glory and incalculable advantages»*. Madrid answered to these demands that, at least for the moment, war was not an advisable option for Spain due to the condition of the Navy, the Army and the Treasury, so that a warlike confrontation in the circumstances might have negative consequences, even for the Americans themselves, to whom —the British fleet dominating the seas— it would not be possible to send the aid they needed so badly for their struggle and, thus, because of this, might be forced to seek peace with the English.

In March 1777, there was a meeting in Burgos between Arthur Lee, brother of General Charles Lee, commanding in Virginia and second to Washington, and the man of confidence of Carlos III, the Marquis of Grimaldi, who had just been replaced at the head of the government by the Count of Floridablanca and who, however, was commissioned for this conference because of his deep knowledge of the negotiations. (Arthur Lee had arrived in Paris months before with Benjamin Franklin and Silas Deane, sent by the American Congress to negotiate with France and Spain; the Spanish Ambassador in Paris, Count of Aranda, held various meetings with Franklin in the French capital). Also at the Burgos meeting was the Bilbao merchant Don Diego de Gardoqui, a competent mediator between the Court and the Americans, and who, in time, would be the first Spanish diplomat accredited to the United States. (The Lee-Grimaldi meeting took place in Burgos and not in Madrid to confuse the British spies.)

Arthur Lee asked the urgent alliance of Carlos III with the new nation, the full recognition of its sovereignty and the immediate intervention of Spain and France in the struggle against England. The reply by Grimaldi was expressive and definitive: «*You have considered your own situation and not ours. The moment has not yet arrived. The war with Portugal, which occupies us now, France being unprepared and our treasure ships not having arrived from South America, does not allow us to make public such an alliance immediately. These reasons will possibly change within a year and then will be the time*».

Grimaldi promised Lee he would increase the Spanish aid to the Americans, which had begun before. In effect, the first donation of Carlos III had amounted to a million pounds, exactly the same amount donated by the King of France. Don Ventura Lloveras, the extraordinary treasurer

56

of Carlos III in Paris, received instructions to deliver to the Spanish Ambassador, the Count of Aranda, four million reales in bullion so that he, in accordance with Vergennes, would see they got to their destination. The above amount was used to purchase 216 bronze cannon, 209 gun-carriages, 27 mortars, 9 fittings, 12,000 boms, 51,000 balls, 300 lots of a thousand pounds of powder, 30,000 rifles with bayonets, 4,000 tents, 30,000 complete uniforms, and lead for rifle balls. These supplies left from French ports and were sent to the United States, via Bermuda, by means of the famous author of «*The Barber of Seville*» and «*The Marriage of Figaro*», and no less famous adventurer, Pedro Carón de Beaumarchais, who had founded the commercial house of «*Rodríguez Hostalé y Compañía*» to carry out this type of operations with the Americans, affairs which, paradoxically, were to lead him to ruin.

In view of what was offered to Lee, instructions were sent to Cuba, announcing the regular shipment of clothing, powder and munitions which should be stored in the Havana warehouses at the disposition of the colonists. In January 1777, there left from La Coruña 9,000 yards of blue cloth, woven in Alcoy, 1,710 of white cloth and 2,992 yards of linsey-woolsey. In the month of February there were sent from the same port two cases of quinine of 920 pounds, two cases of sets of buttons, 100 hundredweight of powder, 300 rifles with bayonets and 14 bales of linsey-woolsey. Other important supplies were accumulated in the ports of Barcelona and Cádiz. It was precisely Diego de Gardoqui who was in charge of organizing the financial and commercial channels for these «exports» by obtaining substantial credits in Lee's favor and the founding of the firm «*Gardoqui e Hijos*», which would see to their destination, as private commercial traffic, the plentiful supplies offered by the Crown. On the other hand, there were turned over to Lee, through Gardoqui, various amounts to acquire merchandise which had to be purchased abroad. Thus, in the month of March he received 3,000 pesos; 50,000 pesos in April; in April, also, 8,100 pounds and, in June, 106,000 in other currency.

After the operations of Lee in Spain, it is Benjamin Franklin who takes the initiative and sends the government of Carlos III a Memorandum in which, at the recommendation of Congress of December 7, 1777, he made the following proposals: 1) The United States would help Spain in the conquest of Pensacola, with the provision that the Americans would have free access to the port and free navigation on the Mississippi. 2) The United States would be willing to declare war on Portugal if Spain so wished. 3) The United States would supply Spain with provisions to the value of two million dollars and 6 frigates of 24-gun, if Spain wished to conquer the Bahamas. There was no Spanish reply to these offers. A little later, the colonists asked Spain for a loan of two million pounds sterling.

Meanwhile the Spanish government, in 1778, had sent to Philadelphia, as unofficial representative to Congress, Don Juan de Miralles, who, close to Washington and Jay, and aware of the various American plans for the invasion of Florida, made the delegates aware of the rights of the Spanish Crown in the reconquest of this province. Later, Miralles would be replaced in his mission by Diego de Gardoqui.

To substitute Arthur Lee, there arrived in Spain, in 1780, John Jay, ex-President of the Congress of the United States. He was accompanied by George Carmichael. He journeyed from Cádiz, where he had landed, to Madrid to hold meetings with the government. He asked, among other help, a loan of one hundred thousand pounds sterling. Jay's negotiations were unsuccessful and, finally, very little satisfied with his activities, and with the doubting atmosphere of the Spanish Court, he left for Paris, in 1782, called by Franklin.

Previously, in the diplomatic interplay, there had been a concrete proposal from the government in London through its Ambassador in Madrid, Lord Grantham. Great Britain was prepared to cede to our country Florida, Gibraltar and the cod-fish banks of Newfoundland, if Spain did not enter the war, closed all its ports to the American rebels and joined forces with the British in subduing the rebels. The reply of Carlos III was completely negative, but it proved the capital importance which the English gave to the Spanish position in the conflict.

In the book «Spain and the Independence of the United States», written by Professor Yela Utrilla, there is included a «Complete record of supplies and costs before September 1777», catalogued in the National Historic Archive in Madrid, in which are detailed, item by item, the acquisitions made by the American Commissioners charged to the credits conceded in Spain to Arthur Lee, and which, for its outstanding documentary interest, we are going to reproduce totally:

«BUDGET»

Balance of Mr. Grand of Amsterdam given on June 10, 1777	664.178.1.1
Payments for August 14, 1777	170.186.11.1
Drafts and orders issued during this time by the commissioners and by Mr. Williams	30.000.0.0
Contract to acquire 30,000 uniforms at 35 pounds each, amounting to	1.050.000.0.0
The same for 1,000 rifles	18.000.0.0
The same for 100 pounds of copper and tin for founding cannon	150.000.0.0
The same for 100 pounds of saltpeter	110.000.0.0
The same for shoes, pistols, etc., acquired by Mr. Williams, including the ship to transport the goods, amounting to	250.000.0.0
Repairs to various boats, amounting to	50.000.0.0
Paid by Mr. Delap of Amsterdam	40.000.0.0
Cordage, anchors, etc., for a 64 gun ship	2.000.000.0.0
To finish and load the ship in Holland there will be needed, as a minimum	550.000.0.0
Received by Mr. Grand on July 10th	500.000.0.0
Debit balance of commissioners per budget ...	1.454.018.10.0
	2.618.196.11.1

Previous balance	1.454.018.10.1
To deliver in October	500.000.0.0
Debit balance of the commissioners after the delivery of 500,000 will be	954.018.10.0
	1.454.018.10.0

Previous balance of 954.010.10 carried over to the next page	954.018.10.0

Blankets, shirts, canvas for tents, bronze cannon and many other essentially necessary items which have not been counted and which amount to a very considerable sum, for example:

80,000 blankets at 7 pounds	560.000.0.0
80,000 shirts at 4 pounds	320.000.0.0
20,000 pairs of shoes at 3.10	70.000.0.0
10,000 «sterkings» (already purchased)	15.000.0.0
70,000 «sterkings» (idem)	105.000.0.0
100 tons of powder (ordered)	200.000.0.0
The sum which the commissioners will owe in October	2.244.018.10

The commissioners have orders to acquire up to 80,000 uniforms, but have only ordered 30,000, lacking to complete the order received.	1.750.000
To supply each soldier with two shirts	320.000
60,000 pairs of shoes	210.000
Harness for 3,000 horses	450.000
The bronze cannon ordered will amount to a minimum of	2.000.000
Adding the cost of transport and costs to each of the products and as these goods must be sent in armed ships, the Congress has ordered the purchase of eight ships of the line, which will cost	3.000.000
All this purchase amounts to	7.730.000

The warships can be purchased at present and the calculated cost is that for paying cash. These ships are absolutely needed both to begin the trade with the transport of the merchandise and war materials acquired, as well as to bring back from America the products needed to pay for them.

The budget does not include many of the necessary articles which the Congress could procure in exchange for its products, in case its commerce were to be protected by eight ships of the line.

This budget, amounting to more than seven million pounds, catalogued in File number 3,884 of the National Historical Archive in Madrid, is sufficiently expressive of the volume of acquisitions of every kind —from ships, cannon and arms to clothing and shoes— charged to the Spanish credits to supply the American armies. Consider, also, that what is detailed here is only one lot of the many which were shipped from Spain and that, on the other hand, regular assistance was supplied from Havana and New Orleans. It can be said, then, Spain shod and dressed the American soldiers, armed their units with the Spanish musket of 1757, then considered the best in the world, supplied with powder and cannon their magazines and artillery and even built and equipped the ships to transport the goods. With reason Helen Auger says that this aid was of great importance to a country «that was as naked and defenseless as an oyster shell». For his part, the investigator Morales Padrón quotes a letter from Benjamin Franklin to the Count of Aranda thanking him effusively for the 12,000 muskets sent to Boston.

Let us set down now two other North American testimonials on this subject. One is that of Bishop Monsignor Fulton Sheen, so famous for his activity on television and for his writings. Here are his words: *«Spain was our friend from the beginning, even before independence was declared. Spain allowed our ships to enter all her ports. The King of Spain gave us 5,000,000 dollars in support of our cause. During 1776 Spain sent us 519 bronze cannon, 30,000 muskets, 35,000 balls, lead, 4,000 tents,*

30,000 uniforms, 1,200 bombs, 200 artillery limbers, and all of it free».

The other opinion is that of Mr. Stanton Griffiths, who was Ambassador of the United States in Spain after the Second World War. The text was published in the daily «Ya» of Madrid on February 5, 1952, and cited a statement by the Ambassador when he disembarked in New York: *«He at once put into historical perspective the present negotiations and alluded to the help Spain gave the United States at the moment of its independence, a fact which the American historians have always tried to hide, or at least to play down, while praising the French aid. They even overlook the fact that Carlos III gave the United States its first loan so as to buy uniforms, munitions and items for its then shirtless army; during fifteen years Spain paid, punctually, one after the other, in the banks of Austria, Germany, Italy and Holland notes which the United States could not honor».*

The most qualified and representative interpreter of this politic of open aid to the Americans was to be Bernardo de Gálvez, from the frontier enclave of Louisiana. The new Governor would have to blend skill with audacity to carry out his objectives, as Spain not being at war with Great Britain, he must, officially, maintain an attitude of neutrality in the conflict. With diligent spirit he set about carrying out his task; the old maxim of the Military Academy —*«si vis pacem para bellum»*— came to his mind. Evidently, the Spaniards knew, and the English, too, that armed conflict between two powerful neighbors with opposing interests was inevitable.

BERNARDO DE GALVEZ

Engraving with the portrait of Bernardo de Gálvez, Count of Gálvez.

Macharavialla (Málaga), birthplace of Bernardo de Gálvez. Original oil by the Spanish painter, Domingo Viladomat, destined for the Gálvez Salon, in Baton Rouge, Louisiana (U. S. A.).

Detail of a typical street in Macharavialla named for New Orleans.

Portrait of José de Gálvez, first Marquis of Sonora, uncle of Bernardo de Gálvez.

Engraving of Don Matías de Gálvez, Viceroy of Mexico, father of Bernardo de Gálvez.

Equestrian portrait of Bernardo de Gálvez.

Engraving of Don Miguel de Gálvez, son of Bernardo de Gálvez.

GOLFO DE MEXICO

...asa del Gobernador.	6. Bahia de Panzacola.
...os Almacenes.	7. Canal de Santa Rosa.
...os Fosos.	8. Ysla de Sta Rosa.
...uerte de Sn Carlos.	9. Punta del Desembarco.

Engraving of the assault on the fortress

DE	11 La Iglesia	16 El Castillo bolado de media.
COLA	12 Trinchera de los Españoles	Se Hallaràen Madrid en la Lib
AIA	13 Desembarco	de la Viuda de Miguel Escribe
Españoles	14 Tropa Españolas	

...ola by the troops of Bernardo de Gálvez.

Praying statue in the Gálvez family pantheon in Macharavialla.

Tomb in which rest the remains of the Marquis of Sonora in Macharavialla.

Praying statues in the pantheon of the Gálvez family.

Coat-of-arms of Bernardo
de Gálvez.

Coat-of-arms of the Gálvez
family of Macharavialla.

Map of the coast of Florida.

Statue of Bernardo de Gálvez, by Juan de Avalos, inugurated by
Juan Carlos I, in Washington.

THE FORGOTTEN ASSISTANCE

During the same days when Arthur Lee was conferring in Burgos with the Marquis of Grimaldi, Gálvez was showing intense activity in Louisiana. He inspected the Indian territories of Natchitoches, Opelusas and Atacapas, reorganized and strengthened the military detachments along the river, made maps of the whole course of the Mississippi and of the coast, and spoke out against illegal trade and fought contraband, by the British.

The first measure of the new Governor, which deeply changed the status of Louisiana, was to declare the port of New Orleans —and all the Spanish ports— open and free to American trade and to admit and to sell the prizes taken by the rebel ships and privateers. This resolution was a hard blow for the British as the Spanish harbors became a refuge for the American ships. The famous Conigham, William Hodges, as well as other corsairs at the service of the colonists, began to use the Spanish ports —Bilbao, La Coruña, Havana, etc.— judging them to be safer than those of France and taking their prizes to them.

The House of Lords itself, in London, reported that in the first twenty months of the war 733 British ships had been captured, which represented a loss of 2,600,000 pounds sterling.

In April of 1777, Gálvez, wishing to suppress all trade with Great Britain, took another decision of great political importance. He captured eleven English ships dedicated to smuggling, as reprisal for the capture by a British warship of three Spanish merchantmen, and immediately decreed that all English subjects must leave Louisiana within fifteen days. This measure, which revolutionized the whole valley of the Mississippi, put once again in the hands of the French the river traffic, previously totally controlled by the British. Faced with the English protests over this measure, Gálvez answered that, in effect, trade on the river was free, but not for contraband.

The blow given by Gálvez had, in reality, a double purpose; for one part, to impress the English, and for the other, to demonstrate to the Americans, before coming events, that, at last, they had in the territory an ally with strength and the capacity for decision.

For his objectives in favoring in so far as possible the American cause, Gálvez counted on the loyal collaboration of an Irishman, Oliver Pollock, a resident of New Orleans who had embraced the rebel cause and soon would be named the official agent of the Congress in Philadelphia. Pollock had earned the confidence of Gálvez's predecessors in the Government, O'Reilly and Unzaga, and had become the most prosperous merchant in the Mississippi Valley. Trading in hides, flour, coffee, sugar, wood, indigo and spices, and with the concession to supply flour to the military detachments along the river, he was considered one of the most solid financiers in the region. He became the personal representative of the important firm of Willing and Morris, of Philadelphia. It was Unzaga himself who recommended him to Gálvez, presenting him as «*a loyal and zealous American in whom he could have absolute confidence*».

Shortly before the arrival of Gálvez in New Orleans, in 1776, General Charles Lee, spokesman for the Security Committee of Virginia, with command over the southern territories to the Mississippi, faced with the difficult time through which the Americans were passing, as the English fleet was blockading the ports to prevent the arrival of arms and supplies, sent an urgent message to the Spanish Governor, Don Luis de Unzaga, through Captain Gibson and Lieutenant Linn, who, commanding a daring group of fifteen men —known as «*Gibson's lambs*»— came down the river river to New Orleans. In his message, from Williamsburg, General Lee urged, «*in the name of humanity*», the delivery by the Mississippi of a shipment of powder, medicines (particularly quinine) and food which would remedy the desperate situation of Fort Pitt —commanded by Colonel Morgan— and other American positions threatened by the English. Lee added every kind of security for the Spanish territories in North America once the colonies had achieved independence.

Unzaga received the messenger secretly and at night to avoid this contact be coming known to the English Consul in New Orleans. Captain Gibson, in speaking, amplified what Lee had written, offering, in the name of Congress the city of Pensacola and other concessions to Spain in compensation for the aid he had come to seek. The Governor was faced with one of those limit-situations which must be solved by a risky personal decision. Given the urgency of the case, and in spite of the «*official*» neutrality of Spain between the two parties, Unzaga, after urgently informing Madrid, resolved to comply with the American petition. Without doubt, he was urged to it by the reports from his detachments at St. Louis, Santa Genoveva, Fort Chartres and on the Ohio announcing a projected offensive by the English forces, with their Indian allies from Illinois, to invade the Lower Mississippi. If Fort Pitt and the other American forts in the region were to fall, the crisis could be extraordinarily serious for New Orleans.

It was Oliver Pollock who took charge of this operation. He chartered a boat and contracted with Unzaa for the purchase of 10,000 pounds of powder from the governmental stores. Under the command of Lieutenant Linn (Captain Gibson remained behind in simulated prison to quiet the suspicions of the English Consul in New Orleans, and later set free) the boat went up river with its precious cargo, the boatmen rowing day and night. The completely exhausted crew reached Fort Arkansas, where the chief of the Spanish detachment gave them shelter and helped them along to the Ohio River. On May 2nd they reached Fort Pitt and the fort was saved thanks to the Spanish powder.

Colonel Morgan, commander of Fort Pitt, wrote to

Gálvez (who had now replaced Unzaga) expressing his gratitude for the opportune delivery of the ten thousand pounds of powder. At the same time he consulted him about the American project to attack Mobile and Pensacola, which appeared practical if they could count on the direct support of the Spanish Governor and the supplying of the American troops from New Orleans with supplies, transport, artillery and powder. In his reply Gálvez said: «*Although it would please me enormously, I can not participate. You may count on my permission and any help it may be possible to give you, but I must appear to be unaware of it all*».

Gálvez and Pollock later perfected this supply system and it functioned satisfactorily. Pollock used his own economic resources to finance these expeditions, risking his personal fortune, and often had available credits generously conceded by Gálvez. Thus, during 1777, the Governor loaned Pollock $ 74,078. One cargo, worth 25,000 gold doubloons, made up of quinine, blankets, shoes, etc., was despatched directly from the government warehouses. The boats sailed under the Spanish flag to avoid the inspections and searches of the British garrison at Fort Natchez and went up the river on journeys which lasted several months, bound for the detachments in the Upper Mississippi and to the frontiers of Virginia and Pennsylvania, from where the supplies were sent to Washington's army and to the southern division of General Lee.

To keep up appearance in the coming and going of the supplies it was necessary, on instructions from Madrid, to give them the character of private commercial operations and Don Eduardo de Miguel was sent from Havana and the deliveries were consigned to him. However, he was soon recognized by the espionage service as a government official and he had to return to Cuba, new ways being found to send the supplies.

In 1778, Pollock purchased, with his own funds, goods to the value of 11,900 golds doubloons which were shipped to Philadelphia to the Committee of Congress. Very expressive is the list of articles which made up this shipment, as recorded by the North American writer James Walton: *«In this cargo, there was in addition to powder, flint-lock rifles, muskets and pistols, horn and marble combs, cups, scissors, razors, butcher knives, hinges, nails, handkerchiefs, flannel thread, tablecloths, napkins, linen, hats, shoes and stockings. Nor was there a lack of items for the «upper» classes, including in the same shipment fine, ruffled shirts, metal buttons, red garters, silk underpants, silver service, wine, cognac and molasses candy».*

THE EXPEDITIONS OF CLARK AND WILLING

The echo of the Spanish help to Fort Pitt, with the intrepid powder expedition, resounded through out the Union and brought a flood of petitions to Gálvez asking for aid of every kind. Among them should be pointed out those of the future Colonel George Rogers Clark, one of the important names of the American rebellion, who was in command of the defense of Kentucky and planned the conquest of Detroit, whose relationship with Pollock and Gálvez became as close as it was decisive. Under Clark's command were famous veterans such as the legendary Daniel Boone, James Harrod and Benjamin Logan.

Clark's campaigns along the Illinois, over several years, in spite of his lack of troops, had great effect on the development of the conflict in the vast regions of the Middle Mississippi, serving as a dam against the wide plotting of the commanders in Detroit. In effect, the English leaders, Hamilton and Stuart, with great resources in money, arms, provisions and gifts, had managed to mobilize a powerful and mercenary army of several thousand Indians from the warlike tribes of the interior, who, punctually bribed with munitions, rum, blankets and scalping-knives, unleashed a bloody and vicious series of raids along the frontier, destroying crops and cabins and butchering entire families of colonists.

In the English Parliament itself, Pitt rose to denounce nobly the ferocious inhumanity of this savage war with indignant words: *«But who is the man who has dared to authorize and associate with our arms the tomahawk a and the scalping-knife of the savages? These crimes wound the sense of honor. It offends me, because I respect war when it is honorable, but I also detest it when it is ruled by criminal barbarity».*

The objective of Hamilton, who received the atrocious help of the *«scalp-buyers»,* was to attack Kentucky and close the Ohio to possible Spanish aid from New Orleans. Clark, understanding the serousness of the situation, conceived the plan of moving ahead of this offensive capturing the English detachments on the Illinois. Once taken Kraskaia, Vincennes and the other forts, he could realize his dream of occupying Detroit and deciding the war in his favor on this wide stage.

Clark presented his plan to the Congress of Virginia asking urgently for men, arms, provisions and money. However, the critical financial position of the Americans, which had reached its lowest point, made it impossible to underwrite Clark's program. The responsibility for supplies and the heavy expenses of the expedition would fall once again on the Governor of Louisiana and on his priceless collaborator, Oliver Pollock. Gálvez, without hesitation, used completely the funds he had available for the maintenance of his province and Pollock, for his part, completely sacrificed his personal fortune, even selling his properties and being at the mercy of his creditors, who put him in prison, from which he was rescued by his friend the Governor; Gálvez himself had to answer for the debts from his personal holdings. Meanwhile, the English General, Sinclair, renewed the plan to conquer the Illinois and St. Louis. Doubling the incentives to the Indians, he organized an expedition in which there was a contingent of Sioux warriors led by the famous Wabasha, the most feared Indian in the territory. This column was to attack the Spanish fort at St. Louis, on the Mississippi. St. Louis was an extraordinarily valuable place, both for its strategic importance, as well as for its economic and rade value, as it was the main center for the fur trade in the Mississippi Valley. Heading the city as Governor was the Spanish Commander Fernando de Leiba, a man of confidence of Gálvez, who had under his orders a tiny garrison: *«Sixteen men, including the drummer-boy, are the forces at my disposal»*, Leiba had written to Gálvez shortly before.

However, St. Louis, reinforced in time by the commander of the fort at Santa Genoveva, Cortabona, with some artillery and by 300 colonists and merchants of the city, among whom was Francisco Vigo, an old Spanish Colonel, retired and dedicated to the fur trade, put up a desperate resistance to the forces of Sinclair who was compelled to call off his attack.

A little later, Clark, helped by supplies from Gálvez and Pollock, who equiped him generously, and by Commander Leiba, who provided a hundred men as reinforcements, began his counted offensive from Fort Pitt. After a terrible march, he fell by surprise on the forts of Kaskaia, Cahokia and Vincennes, whose capture allowed him to dominate the region, frustrate the English designs on Illinois and Kentucky and maintain control of the territories West of the Allegheny Mountains. Clark and Leiba formed a long and friendly relationship, and, even, the American Colonel had a loving and highly novelesque romance with Teresa Leiba, the sister of the Spanish Commander.

Later, with Commander Cruzat in command at St. Louis, and to protect this fort from the British incursions from the North, a small expedition of Spanish soldiers and friendly Indians, under the command of Captain Pourre, was sent against the English detachment at San José on Lake Michigan. San José was taken by surprise, its garrison made prisoner and the booty distributed among the Indians. Here is the text of Pourre's solemn declaration: *«I annex and incorporate into the domains of his Catholic Majesty the King of Spain, my master, for now and forever, this establishment of San José and its dependencies, together with the river of the same name and the Illinois, which flows into the Mississippi...».* In the peace negotiations between Spain and England, this proclamation by Pourre was the basis for the claim to the territory East of the Mississippi by the Spaniards.

A very controversial episode was that featuring James

Willing, *«Captain in the service of the Independent United States of America»*. Willing, aboard the armed ship *«Rattletrap»*, and at the head of a small troop of adventurers, came down the Mississippi, sacking, burning and destroying the British settlements and Indian villages along the river, forcing the mass flight of their inhabitants, who, terror-stricken, took refuge in the capital of Louisiana under the shelter of Gálvez's authority, and provoking protests to the Governor by the British representatives because of the damages inflicted and the presence of Willing in New Orleans. Bernardo acted with skill, demanding a statement of neutrality from all the refugees, confiscating the booty collected by Willing, selling it at public action and indemnifying the victims, as well as sending the predator back home, measures which tried to alleviate the disaster caused by Willing's actions, avoiding a chain of reprisal and vengeance against the Americans and, on the rebound, against the Spaniards.

WEDDING IN NEW ORLEANS

On December 2, 1777, Bernardo married María Feliciana de Saint-Maxent. It was an ominous wedding with
neither celebrations nor solemnities. It was held in the
Governor's home, in secret, as Gálvez did not have the
Royal permission, which as military commander he needed.
He was at the time gravely ill and, faced possibly with
death, he wished to honor the word he had given. That
is the reason for the urgency of the sacrament, which was
given, *«in articulo mortis»* and ommitting the rite, by
Fray Cirilo de Barcelona, Vicar General and priest of the
parish of San Luis of New Orleans. Once the Governor
had recovered his health, the King's permission arrived
and the wedding was made public *«so that there should
never be any doubt as to its legitimacy»*.

María Feliciana de Saint-Maxent known in New Orleans
for her extraordinary charm. *«As beautiful as she was
loved by all»*, according to the testimony of Humboldt,
she was the widow of Don Juan Bautista d'Estrehán (from
which marriage she had a daughter Adelaida), and daughter

of Don Gilberto Antonio de Saint-Maxent, both of French origin, belonging to families of the high society of Louisiana and addicted to the cause of Spain. D'Estrehán had been the Treasurer of the King of France in New Orleans and creator of the first sugar-mill in the province; Saint-Maxent was from Brandenburg, of noble family. Becoming rich in the fur trade with the Indians, he had given outstanding service to the previous Governors of the province, Don Antonio de Ulloa and Don Alejandro O'Reilly, at the time of a frustrated rebellion of the French colonists against Spain, for which he was richly rewarded by O'Reilly, who got for him the nomination as Captain of the Militia Infantry of New Orleans, with the consent of Carlos III. María Feliciana was celebrated for her overwhelming sympathy and attractiveness and wove with Gálvez, throughout their marriage, what has been called a «romantic idyll». They had three children: Matilde, Miguel and Guadalupe, this last born in Mexico just days after Bernard's death.

It was not only Gálvez. Many other Spanish officers fell equally fascinated before the witchery of the beautiful girls of New Orleans. Thus, Lieutenant Jacinto Panis, married Margarita Wiltz, also a widow, and Esteban Miró, Commander of the Battalion of Louisiana, fell passionately in love with on of the official beauties of the city, María Celeste Eleonora de Macarty. In addition, the three older sisters of María Feliciana also married Spaniards. Isabel, the first-born, married Don Luis de Unzaga; Mariana married Don Manuel de Flon, Count of La Cadena, of Gálvez's army, and Victoria married Don Juan Antonio

Riaño, who was at the siege of Pensacola. Thus we have the curious circumstance that three successive Governors of Spain in Louisiana, Don Luis de Unzaga, Don Bernardo de Gálvez and Don Esteban Miró, were married to Creoles from New Orleans.

The popularity of Gálvez in the city, sustained by his open and happy character, by his audacity and youth, by the prestige of his previous military history and by his knowledge of French, increased after this fortunate marriage to a Creole highly admired in the city, a marriage which, linking him intimately to Louisiana, encouraged, without doubt, the feelings of the natives of the country, who, from then on, considered Gálvez as one of their own and gave him their support without reserve.

Everything smiled on the young couple. Life in New Orleans was a festival, the crossroad of races and cultures, key to the Gulf of Mexico and gateway to America. Clearly Latin in appearance —New Orleans was founded in 1718 by Bienville and named in honor of the Regent of France, the Duke d'Orleans— its French origin blended harmoniously with its Spanish present in a brilliant and busy setting of traders, hunters, trappers, Indians who lived along the river —the Creeks, Chickasaws, Seminoles— blacks from the immense plantations of the Mississippi and the Missouri, French, Spanish, Creoles... A fascinating enclave and at peace on the flank of the war between Americans and British.

There is a stereotyped image of the New Orleans of those days which has come down to us intact, like a romantic cliche, in literature and motion pictures, even in architecture and music, as a world closed in on itself, which begins and ends in itself, set in genuine and unchangeable scenes in films such as «Gone with the Wind»: mansions set in gardens among giant, moss-covered trees, and in whose sumptuous salons there were parties and balls with all the refinements of Europe, while guitars, banjos and violins played, and in the harbor district there were blended the songs of the divermen and the primitive «blues» under the warm nights of Louisiana, in the magic of the South.

A city, in sum, with personality and style, which imitated the fashions and customs of the Courts of Madrid and Versailles. Under the Spanish government New Orleans prospered rapidly and at the beginning of the 19th century rivalled Philadelphia, at the time the most important capital of the new United States.

Even today, New Orleans preserves a marked Latin air, where it is hard to distinguish the French from the Spanish. The famous Vieux Carré district, the heart of the city, belongs to the Spanish architectural tradition, with its typical galleries and forged-iron grilles. Completely Spanish are the Cabildo, built in 1795 by the wealthy Spaniard Andrés de Almonaster, the former general headquarters of the Governor of Louisiana, and the Presbitery. Great works were undertaken then; such as the system of fortifications and the Carondelet Canal, public lighting was installed and the Saint Louis Cathedral was built. Don Francisco Luis Héctor, Baron of Carondelet, built the first theater in New Orleans, one of the most important streets in the city bears the name of this Spanish Governor, and another that of Gálvez. Recently there was inaugurated the great Plaza of Spain.

During the forty years of Spanish domination —as never before— there was seen the flourishing of Louisiana. The population grew from 10,000 to 50,000. Gálvez, and his successors, promoted immigration and brought from Spain groups of colonists who transformed great expanses of virgin land into fertile tobacco and sugar-cane plantations. In 1778 there arrived 1,582 immigrants from the Canaries who made various settlements on the banks of the river *(Valenzuela, Tierra del Buey* and *Barataria)* and, a year later, there came 500 from Málaga, countrymen of Bernardo, who founded New Iberia in the bayou regions. Each family was given a house, cattle, fowl, tools and a ration for four years. Meanwhile, American refugees built a town to the Northwest of New Orleans, at the mouth of the Amite River which, in honor of the Governor, they named Galveztown. In homage to the wife of Gálvez they gave the name of Feliciana to a town (divided into the parishes of East and West Feliciana) which still exist. Another town bore the name of New Feliciana. Cities also of Spanish origin are Opelousas, to the North of New Iberia, and Los Adaes, the old site of a religious mission which, for fifty years, was the capital of the province of Texas.

Until just a short while ago there was still preserved (and it has not been lost completely) the Spanish language, fused with English and American influences, in these nuclei of old Louisiana, as revealed by Carlos Fernández-

Shaw in his work *«The Spanish Presence in the United States»*.

It was Oliver Pollock who expressed the wish that a portrait of the Governor should be hung in the Congress *«to perpetuate your memory in the United States of America, as being known in your sublime nation as a great soldier and gentleman, you have performed a great service in the conquest of liberty.»* According to various testimonies, it was customary to toast at banquets the Generals Washington and Gálvez. Also, in the coinage. With reason writes Aaron Trager that the American dollar sign is inherited from the «real de a ocho» of Spain. In fact, the popular $ sign is a survivor of the legend —Plus Ultra (Further)— which is blazoned on the Pillars of Hercules of our escutcheon. The first issues of paper money by the Americans were backed by the guarantee of Spanish currency. One of the first bank-notes, dated in October of 1776, that is to say, immediately after the Declaration of Independence, shows clearly this statement: *«Eight Spanish Milled Dollars»*. And the same for those of three and twenty dollars. The bank-note issued by the Richmond Corporation reproduces, in a highly visible place, the reverse side of a *«real de a ocho»* which shows the crest of Spain. Lastly, the word *«dollar»* is derived directly from the Spanish *«dobla»*, that is, from the coin of that name.

The exceptional qualities of Gálvez as a diplomat were amply demonstrated in his maintenance of the difficult Spanish position under a cape of apparent *«official»* neutrality between the English and the Americans, having, however, to cover up *«real»* assistance to the rebels; there were also confirmed his abilities as an organizer with the vast political plan which had for its setting the valley of the Mississippi, and his vision and resourcefulness as a statesman in promoting the economic and commercial development of the province and its growth in population as the basic condition for immediate prosperity; he was capable of building, in sum, excellent public relations with the racial communities of Louisiana and especially, with the Indian tribes. On one critical occasion, there appeared in the Governor's Palace in New Orleans 17 Choctaw chiefs, who threw at the feet of Gálvez the British flags and medals they had received as tokens of alliance with the British, which obligation they now wished to bread. Gálvez gave them 17 silver medals of the same size, with the figure of Carlos III.

Without doubt, Gálvez made all aware of his human, modern, progressive and liberal character. Now he was called upon to revalidate his qualities as a military leader, as a man of war, but this was, evidently, his own playing-field.

THE GREAT MARCH UP THE MISSISSIPPI

All the news coincided in the Summer of 1779. The English were hurriedly preparing the invasion of Louisiana and a crushing attack on New Orleans, through the massing of their forces in Canada and Florida with the object of achieving the definitive domination of the valley of the Mississippi and strangling the rebellion, which obviously, and in good part, was being maintained by Spanish aid, as was proven by recent successes of Clark. The war, thus, was moving its center of gravity from the North to the South.

Faced with the urgency of the situation, Gálvez called, with extraordinary character, a meeting of his Military Council. There attended all the chiefs of the Spanish forts and districts in the Mississippi Valley and the frontier with Florida: attending were all the experienced Captains, Cruzat, who came from his detachment at St. Louis; Juan de la Villebreuve, from the southern border on the route to Pensacola; Alejandro Coussot, who was in command of the Arkansas district, and the other Captains, Pedro José

Favrot, Hilario de Estenoy, Joaquín de Blanca, Manuel de Nava and Martín Mozún, all detachment commanders. And together with them, the senior officers in Louisiana: Colonel Manuel González and the Lieutenant-Colonels Esteban Miró and Pedro Piernas, acting as Secretary of the Council Commander Jacinto Panis, recently arrived from a secret mission in Pensacola.

The Governor reported on the messages to the English garrisons which had been intercepted, as well as on information received from other sources, which confirmed the British preparations, their equipment and activities for an immediate outbreak of hostilities; also, on the fact that 400 Walloon Guards had reinforced the fort at Manchak. The whole military apparatus of Great Britain, from Montreal to Pensacola, in league with the Indian hordes of the Iroquois and the Sioux, was being mobilized for a full offensive against New Orleans.

The Council decided to concentrate in the city all the soldiers and means of defense available, leaving the forts ungarrisoned, and ask for urgent help from Havana. The preparations were begun immediately, but a furious storm swept across the region a few days later and sunk all the boats in the Mississippi. In a letter to his uncle, José, the Minister of the Indies, Gálvez told of the effects of the hurricane: «... *for leagues around all is in ruins, the crops lost, the trees uprooted, the men overwhelmed, their wives and children scattered through the desert fields exposed to the weather, the land flooded and all sunk in the river, together with my resources, asistance and hopes...*».

At the same time, Gálvez received despatches from the Captain General of Havana informing him of the declaration of war between Spain and England, officially agreed by the government in Madrid. Bernardo kept this news army nor the city, undoubtedly to gain time and move to himself, informing no one for the moment, neither his before the British in the strategy he was planning. At the same time, Bernardo was confirmed as effective Governor of Louisiana with full powers, as until then he had been acting only on an interim basis.

Gálvez then called together the whole population of New Orleans in a great assembly and told them that Spain had been declared an enemy by England *as a consequence of the recognition of American independence*. He explained the weakness of the forces of Louisiana against the imminent attack expected from the English and asked for volunteers. With his well-known oratorical skill, he told the citizens: *«I can not take possession of my office of Governor without swearing before the City Council that I will defend the province; but, although I am ready to shed the last drop of my blood for Louisiana and for my King, I can not take an oath which I might have to violate, because I do not know if you will help me to resist the ambitious designs of the British. What do you say? Shall I take the oath as Governor? Shall I swear to defend Louisiana?»*

The reaction was unanimous. Juan Antonio Gayarre, Chief of the War Commisariat and spokesman for the people of New Orleans, answered in the name of all: *«Take the oath; for the defense of Louisiana and in the*

*service of the King, we offer you out lives and would
offer you our fortunes if we had any left».*

Having achieved the adhesion of the people, the Governor feverishly speeded up his preparations. Gálvez
decided, against the judgement of some officers of the
Council, in favor of remaining on the defensive, that the
only way he had to save Louisiana was to launch a
surprise attack on the British forts on the Mississippi.
Moving before the enemy and taking him by surprise was
the only card he had to play. And he decided to play
it without losing a single day, convinced that attack was
the best defense. Four boats were raised from the river-
bed and equipped with the ten cannons which defended
New Orleans. Other ships were requisitioned along the
coast.

Having collected all the forces at his disposition, the
expedition took two routes. The fleet, under the command
of Julián Alvarez, an expert artillery officer, although
very ill, went up the Mississippi, while by land Gálvez
placed himself at the head of a column made up of 170
veteran soldiers, 330 recruits, 20 carbiniers, 60 militiamen
and citizens of New Orleans, 8 free blacks and 67 American volunteers, among them Oliver Pollock, who acted as
aide-de-camp to Gálvez. Along the way, in the German
settlement of Acadia, and in those of Opelusas, Atacapas
and Punta Cortada, he collected another 600 men, the
majority Germans, as well as 160 Indians and another
group of blacks and mulattos. The whole came to a
total of 1,450 men.

It was the first time that a military expedition had been made up, shoulder to shoulder, of whites, Indians and blacks; and amongs the whites, French, Spaniards, Germans, Americans, Creoles... How could such a heterogeneous group be blended into a true army, with morale and training, organized and efficient? These were the worries of Gálvez and his officers. For the moment, the Governor had no other option than to lead his motley host in forced marches against time. The column, without tents or baggage, advanced painfully, crossing forests and swamps with heavy losses, and after eleven days on the march they came to the fort at Manchak, the first objective of the campaign. This was the moment that Gálvez chose to reveal to his troops that Spain and England were at war and that he had received orders to occupy the British posts on the Mississippi. The soldiers received the news with enthusiasm.

Manchak was taken by assualt on September 7th, the English surrendering and the garrison taken prisoner. The first man to enter the fort, by a loophole, was Gilberto Antonio de Saint-Maxent. The victory, although of small proportions, had the virtue of raising the morale and confidence of the troops and encourage them for the new actions they faced. After a few short days of rest to recover strength, Gálvez led them against the fort at Baton Rouge, defended by a moat with 18 cannon and 600 men under the command of the English Colonel Dickson. The attack on Baton Rouge, which was solidly defended, presented tactical military problems infinitely superior to those at Manchak. Gálvez, who managed to block a rescue column to Baton Rouge from Pensacola, was conscious that he could not risk a siege of several months, as his army would disintegrate. On the other hand, neither was he prepared to sacrifice a great number of lives in a frontal attack on the fort in which the English would have all the advantages.

Thus, he turned to a skillful strategy. He decided to dig silently a trench to be able to use the artillery. All night the sappers worked in silence. Meanwhile, another patrol, screened by trees, pretended to construct ramparts and fired their arms to attract the attention of the fort's artillery. While the English shelled the woods without injuring a single man, the artillerymen mounted their batteries with musket-shot of the fort. At dawn the cannons of Julián Alvarez opened fire on the fort until the destruction was so complete that Colonel Dickson, at three in the afternoon, had to capitulate, surrendering not only Baton Rouge, but also the fort at Pan Mure, in Natchez, with a garrison of 80 Grenadiers, as Gálvez demanded.

This is how Gálvez wrote to his uncle, José, about this battle, on October 16, 1779, according to the report which is preserved in the Archive of Simancas: «*After a truce to bury the dead, the survivors left the fort with full military honors; 375 regular troops laid down their arms, hauled down their flags and were made prisoners. The civilians and blacks were left at liberty to return to their homes with the promise of remaining neutral. The regular troops, now prisoners, were left under the guard of four cadets, while the main body of the troops entered and took possession of the fort. At the same time, a Captain, Juan de Villebreuve, with 50 men, was sent to occupy Pan Mure and Natchez, a victory which was very satisfying, as the high walls around this outpost would have made its conquest very difficult».*

In effect, on October 5th, Juan de Villebreuve received from Captain Forster, who was in command, the surrender of Pan Mure and Natchez. He was the bearer of a letter from Oliver Pollock for the inhabitants of Natchez which is worth quoting: *«Colonel Dickson has capitulated to Governor Gálvez and surrendered his garrison; he has ordered the with drawal of your forces and has delivered the fort to the Spanish officer commissioned for that purpose. The spirit of liberty, the protection which every American has received on this river from His Excellency Governor Gálvez, his generous conduct towards all the inhabitants, with the advantages which should now arise from uninterrupted trade with New Orleans, where you will find a good market for your products and the necessary supplies for your families, I hope will be more than sufficient encouragement for you to render all services within your means to the arms of His Catholic Majesty».*

Only days after the occupation of the fort by the Spaniards, news reached Natchez from the English commander at Pensacola advising them officially of the declaration of war between England and Spain and giving instructions for the projected British attack on New Orleans. The events proved Gálvez was right in having kept that news secret, a fact which allowed him to move before the enemy and incline the surprise factor to his side.

Meanwhile, a group of civilian volunteers from New Orleans, concretely the Pointe Coupée, commanded by Carlos Gran Pré, occupied the English outposts between the Thomson Creeks and the banks of the Amite. Gálvez rewarded him by naming him commander of that district. For his part, Sergeant Juan Bautista Menzinger, with some veteran soldiers, captured two British boats in the Amite River, and a young and intrepid American ally, Captain Robert Pickles, on board the corvette *«Morris»*, captured the English barentine *«West Florida»*, which he rebaptized with the name of *«Galveztown»*, and which would play an outstanding role in the capture of Pensacola. Another small Spanish ship, commanded by Vicente Rillieux, sighted a well-armed British transport which was sailing to Manchak and had the good fortune to take it as a prize by a skillful strategy, opening fire on it and capturing the whole crew. *«To his great surprise»* —wrote Gálvez— *«he found 56 soldiers of the Waldek Regiment and 10 or 12 sailors, all taken prisoner by just 14 Creoles under the command of Rillieux»*.

The first phase of the war had ended. Gálvez's army, with hardly any losses, returned to New Orleans. On January 10, 1780, there arrived a solemn note from Carlos III congratulating them on *«the happy success of the expedition carried out with such spirit and speed by the Governor and his men and the great valor and courage shown by their scanty forces»*. As a reward for his victories,

Gálvez was promoted to Brigadier. But the rewards were not only for him. Bernardo, in his personal reports to the King, always through his uncle, José, had taken particular care to reflect the merits shown in heroic actions by his soldiers, without distinction of rank or race, and giving the names and concrete details of the personal acts to which could be attributed a good part of the success achieved.

Thus, in the recent operations on the Lower Mississippi, he placed before Madrid, with great psychological and political intuition, the conduct of the German volunteer militia from Acadia who, in spite of having been istreated by the English over a long period of time, were an example not only of courage, but of discipline at the victory; Gálvez underlined also the companies of blacks and mulattos, *«who had performed with the same courage and bravery as the white troops»* and who were now rewarded by the King, agreeing to the proposal of the Governor, with 32 Royal Medals for Merit in the Field; also the object of distinctions were the Indians, who, under the influence of Santiago Trascón and José Sorolle, of the Opelousas, conducted themselves correctly under their Spanish leaders; all those who merited it were named individually, and many, including Oliver Pollock, Lieutenant Vicente Rillieux and Captain Pickles, among others, received promotions or decorations from Carlos III. This consideration of Gálvez for those who had helped him so greatly was, without doubt, a determining factor in maintaining the cohesion, discipline and morale of a highly heterogeneous army and which, in great part, had practically been improvised on the battlefield.

In four weeks they had occupied three forts, taken prisoner 570 regular soldiers and captured eight ships, dominating the lower basin of the Mississippi, expelling the British from it and frustrating the enemy's plans to attack down the river from Canada. In reality, the importance of the lightning campaign of Gálvez was in having opened a *«second front»* and making obligatory the presence of important English forces in Florida, with the consequent relief for the Americans. For an exact understanding of the matter, we transcribe the following paragraph from Parker: *«For the second time the young Hawk of Spain had gone into action in the North of the American continent in a way that would have a profound effect on the struggling nation. Again, the General Government in Philadelphia failed in not recognizing its great debt to its defender and friend in the Mississippi Valley».*

After the lightning march of Gálvez up the great river, the war changed scenes. From Louisiana it moved to Florida, where the English held two important fortresses of great strategic value in the domination of the Gulf of Mexico and which were, at the same time, the most important places in the province: Mobile and Pensacola.

THE SPANIARDS AND FLORIDA

Florida held many memories for the Spaniards, as not for nothing has it been discovered by Juan Ponce de León, in 1513, when he arrived on the continent, driven, according to legend, by the Faustian dream of the man in search of the *«Fountain of Youth»*. Ponce de León (companion of Columbus on his second voyage) gave this land the name it still bears, as he found it on Easter Sunday (the *«Pascua Florida»*).

Here was founded the first North American city, San Agustín de la Florida, founded by Governor Menéndez de Avilés, in 1565. Here, in the oldest Mission in the New World, that of Nombre de Dios, Father Francisco López de Mendoza said the first Mass on the continent. Menéndez de Avilés brought a thousand Spanish colonists and also livestock and plants; oranges, figs, sugar-cane, while the Franciscans built 34 missions along the coast, from St. Augustine to Catalina Island, in Georgia, and Father Alonso de Reynoso was called the *«Fray Junípero Serra of the Atlantic»*.

Now, under Gálvez, the Spaniards returned to Florida, the province that Carlos III had to cede to England a short time before, as a result of the treaty which put an end to the Seven Years War. Of the two main objectives of the war which was now being renewed —the recovery of Florida and the conquest of Gibraltar— one was now within hand's reach. His forces reorganized, Gálvez started his march again, seeking to give Mobile and Pensacola the decisive blow to the English power in the Gulf of Mexico.

In his office in the Council of the Indies, in Madrid, José de Gálvez, Minister of Carlos III, opened the mail he had just received from distant Florida and read, impatiently, the report, written in his own hand, from his nephew Bernardo, with the description of the actions carried out by his forces before the fortress of Mobile.

«Today I have the satisfaction of informing you of how, four days after digging the trench, the fortress of Mobile, with the 300 men who defended it, has surrendered to the forces of the King and have been taken prisoner, together with a large cannon and eight mortars. This action has caused us some losses. The resistance was energetic and although this increases the merit of the victory of our tired troops, poorly dressed and saved from shipwreck, there is another circumstance which I feel you shoul bring to the attention of His Majesty».

«That is, that after the news of our shipwreck, General Campbell decided to leave a small garrison in Pensacola and come to attack us by land with the greater part of his forces so as to settle on this field the destiny of the

province. He came with 1,100 men to within almost nine leagues of our camp. You will understand our situation, with our food supplies nearly exhausted, with very little ammunition —as the greater part was lost in the shipwreck— and with 1,100 of the enemy in sight, whose General had ordered them to fix bayonets, plus 300 men in the fort, giving General Campbell 1,400, the same as ourselves, but with the country on their side and the protection of the fort. Such a disagreeable perspective did not weaken in the least the confidence and hope of victory of our troops. On the contrary, believing that greater efforts were needed, they persevered in their tasks, dug the trench, placed the battery and attacked and conquered the fort within view of the vanguard of General Campbell, who settled for watching us. For eight days he was witness to the valor and gallantry of our troops, which made him change his opinion, strike his camp and return to Pensacola with his army, on whose rearguard fell one of our patrols, taking prisoner a Captain and 20 men».

«I can not express the feelings of my small army when they saw the withdrawal of General Campbell without facing us; nor can I reflect their sadness on seeing that the reinforcements from Havana had not arrived in time for us to launch an attack on the enemy and thus triumph over the English as at Saratoga».

«I know you will read with the same feelings as I describe it the news of having lost an opportunity which would have given us Pensacola with the corresponding glory this would have meant for our country; but, at the *same time I have the pleasure of assuring you that all the officers and troops have no other desire than to continuing proving to His Majesty their resolution in sacrificing themselves in his service. I leave for another occasion, due to lack of time, the list of those who should be commended to his royal grace».* In reality, little can be added to the clear description by Bernardo of the capture of Mobile, the second English establishment in importance in the Southeast. It was 10 in the morning on August 14, 1780, when the English flag was lowered in view of the city and, Commander Durnford having surrendered, the Spanish flag was raised over Fort Charlotte. Gálvez had under his command, sent from Cuba, some veterans of the Spanish Infantry Regiment, the Prince's Battalion, the Fixed Battalion of Havana and the Batallion of Louisiana.

There should be amplified, however, this last line of Bernardo's report in which he refers to *«the list of those who should be recommended to his royal grace».* Gálvez remained faithful to his norm of detailing for the government in Madrid, and without favoritism because of race or social position, the courage of those men for whom he asked from the King, in strict justice, concrete reward. Thus, he proposed a decoration for Isidro Roig, of the veteran Cantabrian Regiment, *«who distinguished himself gloriously in defending a settlement against the attack of 200 English soldiers and 500 Indian allies after receiving innumerable wounds which caused his death».* Gálvez asked the decoration for the son of Roig, still only a child, with the payment to go to the widow as long as she should live. In the same action, and at his side, there fell Lieutenant Marcelino de Córdoba. Gálvez asked that his young brother, a Cadet Sub-Lieutenant, «*should be promoted to his brother's rank because of his courageaous conduct in the same action*». In it he had fought desperately over the stabbed body of his brother, keeping the Indians from mutilating it. Gálvez asked that the pay of the dead brother should be continued to the mother of the young officer «*as she has small children, who in their day will also serve the King, continuing the tradition of the ancient house of the Córdoba*».

In another report, Gálvez asked life pensions for two volunteer soldiers of the batallion of Louisiana Militia, Juan Herbert and Maturino Laundry, «*who fought for three days, were mutilated for life and left for dead in the attacks of the savages, who moved through the deep forests as silent and innumerable as the leaves of the trees. Through these terrible days and nights, these two men, badly injured, moved from one side to the other of the swampy terrain as softly as animals, without leaving a trace because of their intimate knowledge of the place. Their orientation in the forests, up to their knees in snake-infested ponds, their familiarity with the sounds of these dark places, saved the tiny unit, which without their help would have fallen victim to the silent and deadly knives of the Indians*». Gálvez asked for these heroic soldiers the promotion to the effective grade of Sergeant, with full pay for life for that grade.

He also asked His Majesty that Enrique Desporez, Captain of the Militia of the Regiment of New Orleans, be given a full promotion to Lieutenant of Infantry, with standing as a career officer, with the possibility of transfer to the regular forces in Mexico so that he could perfect his military training, because of his heroic conduct in the Battle of Mobile. Gálvez sums up one of his reports by pointing out that, in spite of his now long experience as a soldier, in which he had fought for the King in numerous campaigns, with the scars of several wounds, he had never before seen such a chilling series of heroic deeds, misery, sacrifice and suffering as on this frontier.

Carlos III showed the young leader a new sign of his royal appreciation, ordering his promotion to Field Marshal, naming him Governor of Louisiana and Mobile and recognizing his supreme jurisdiction over the military forces of Spain in America, both on land and on sea. The King previously, heading off possible objections, had set forth the reasons which justified the selection of Bernardo over, even, senior officers of Mexico or Cuba for the command of the operations in Florida, which were based on the following motives: He knew well both the setting where the operations would take place and the enemy, with whom he had been in contact previously in the battles of the Mississippi, he had won the friendship and collaboration of the Choctaw Indians and he had the confidence of the American Congress.

Meanwhile, in his office in the Council of the Indies, after reading the report from his nephew on the capture of Mobile, took up his pen and wrote to Bernardo: *«Truthfully, the capture of an important town, fortified and defen-*

ded with courage, is a praiseworthy act, but it is even more worthy of praise when this deed is carried out with insufficient forces, recently rescued from two shipwrecks, almost without food and depressed by fatigue, and still more so when the attack was carried out within sight of a superior force...».

THE UNFINISHED CATHEDRAL

For the total domination of the Gulf of Mexico it was still necessary to take Pensacola. The city, well-fortified, defended by the castle of St. George and the artillery of the Barrancas Coloradas bastion on the tiny island of Santa Rosa, which guarded its well-sheltered bay, was defended by General John Campbell, under the orders of General Peter Chester, Governor and Commander-in-Chief, Vice-Admiral of his Britannic Majesty in the province of West Florida.

After the loss of Mobile, the English command considerably reinforced the garrison of Pensacola, to which were also added large contingents of Indian warriors, whose open use in the field had always been opposed by Gálvez, as is confirmed by this communication which he sent, uselessly, to Campbell: «*The Indians who support the English cause believe they are performing a service by destroying all the inhabitants of my nation. Those who embrace our cause believe they can commit the same acts against the subjects of your Monarch. In this war which we are waging out of a sense of duty and not of hatred, I hope that Your Excellency will be inclined to join me in a reciprocal agreement which will protect us against the horrible criticism of inhumanity».*

Gálvez was conscious of the difficulties of the attack on the British fortress. Always looking ahead, two years before, in 1778, he had sent Captain Jacinto Panis to Pensacola, apparently on an official mission to General Chester, who received him in the gentlemanly way of the period. In reality, Panis's mission was to study secretly, on the spot, the system of fortifications, its possibilities for defense and the location of the harbor, powder magazines and warehouses. The data obtained by this mission of Panis were valuable to the tactical plan Gálvez was preparing.

Bernardo resolved to attack Pensacola by sea and not by land; for this he would need a well-equipped fleet, which he asked for insistently from the Captain-Generalcy of Havana. However, in Cuba, the commanders of the Navy showed themselves lacking in confidence, reticent and in disagreement with Gálvez's strategy The naval chief himself, Don Miguel de Goicoechea, reported to the Council of Havana that the best means to conquer the place was by an advance on land towards the Perdido River. Gálvez answered with asperity: *«The project you have indicated to attack Pensacola along the Perdido River is impracticable. God willing that all were as you have reported, but, unfortunately, there is a great difference between the description and the reality».* There grew up, thus, a series of differences, delays and obstacles between the military commanders in Cuba and Gálvez, which slowed down considerably the operations against Pensacola, and because of which even the King had to show his displeasure and preoccupation. Finally, Gálvez decided to go to Havana to try to convince the War Board of the necessity to face the coming offensive with resolution.

Meanwhile, in Spain, the echoes of the victories on the Mississippi and in Florida had excited the country and all its energies and military efforts were dedicated to the task of supplying troops and provisions for America. The name of Gálvez was a symbol to the enthusiasm of the youth. Innumerable officers and volunteers enlisted in the fleet which was being prepared in Cádiz to assist Gálvez in his final assault. Covered to excess the available places, the aspiring volunteers resorted to every kind of trick and procedure to find a place in the expedition.

The cities rivalled one another in collecting funds, clothing, medicines and arms to equip the ships. The old Malaguenian traditions tell —and, at least, so it has passed into legend— that at the time there being under construction the twin towers of the Cathedral of Málaga (planned in the 16th century by Diego de Siloé), one of them could not be completed because the money assigned for it was ceded to the public subscription for the fleet. There were ships, but the Cathedral lost one of its towers. The completed tower, the only one the magnificent church has, was inaugurated on August 3, 1779, as is certified by an inscription on a tile at the entrance to the Cathedral. Of the other tower we can only see the stumps of the columns which were to flank the campanile.

This is, however, a page which is still not completely clarified. The version most fully approaching reality may be this other. The works of the Cathedral of Málaga were paid for by charges to a tax —an *«Arbitrio de Aduanas»*— awarded by Carlos III for that purpose and consisting of half a *«real»*, later a quarter of a *«real»*, for each 25 pounds of fruit (grapes, raisin or wine) exported from the ports of Málaga and Marbella, and also from Vélez-Málaga. Given the situation and the events we are commenting on, the Council of the Cathedral stopped receiving this tax (which went, in truth, to enlarge the collections for the Gálvez expedition), and the works were interrupted while the right-hand tower was still not finished. Since then the Cathedral has been known affectionately to the Malaguenians as the *«one-armed»*. In any case, it appears clear that the Cathedral of Málaga was a *«victim»*, at long-range, of the American war for independence.

And not only in metropolitan Spain. Thousands of miles away, almost halfway around the world, on the West coast of the Pacific Ocean —at that time from point to point a Spanish sea, a *«mare nostrum»*— the inhabitants of the primitive settlements cooperated as well in the war in Louisiana and Florida which was to have such a profound influence on the struggle for independence of the colonies. At the initiative of the *«father and founder of California»*, Fray Junípero Serra, the missions contributed two pesos for each Spaniard and one for each Indian. The amount collected was delivered to the Viceroy of New Spain, who, in his turn, sent it to General Rochambeau.

This donation from the Spanish missions in California to the war, in favor of the liberty of the Americans, meant, certainly, the first gesture of solidarity on the North American continent, a precocious testimony of brotherhood between the shores of the two great oceans —the Pacific and the Atlantic— long before the foundational project of the United States was consolidated.

Another profile of this vast assistance movement was represented by private Cuban contributions at a critical moment for the military situation of the rebels when, with the collapse of the financial resources of the financier of the Revolution, Robert Morris, and his inability to obtain new credits, the French General Rochambeau, told the Admiral of the same nationality, De Grasse, allies of the Americans, that he could not answer for his troops if they were not paid immediately. De Grasse offered to make an effort in Santo Domingo, an island in which he had connections. On board the frigate *«Aigrette»* he went to Haiti, but there his efforts to collect the large amount needed by the Army, 1,200,000 pounds, were useless. The frigate then sailed to Cuba, where the French delegate, Saint-Simon, had connections to the new Governor of the island and with his aide-de-camp, Don Francisco de Miranda, *«The Precursor»*, who would later play an important role in the independence movements in South America. Through the *«Women's Committees of Havana»*, which promoted numerous associations and schools, they managed, with the contributions of the colonists, merchants and tobacco traders of Cuba, to collect —part in diamonds and other jewels and part in gold coins— the amount needed by Rochambeau, that is, 1,200,000 pounds. This sum played an important part in the final phase of the campaign which ended in the surrender of Cornwallis to Washington at Yorktown.

Also, from the Spanish Viceroyalties in Mexico, Lima and Buenos Aires, and, even, from the Philipines, in a Spanish solidarity movement, there was a mobilization of resources to assist the campaign in Florida. Meanwhile, Gálvez was struggling in Havana with the Governor, Diego Navarro, and with the Commanding General, Navia. At last he was able to convince them and the War Board, headed by Navarro, and with the assistance of Don Juan Bautista Bonet and Don Guillermo Waugham, it authorized 3,800 men to sail under his command with provisions for six months, in addition to another 2,000 soldiers from Mexico and Campeche and all which might be collected in Puerto Rico and Santo Domingo.

On October 16, 1780, while the bells of Havana rang out and there were prayers in all the churches, the fleet set sail for the continent. Between October 18th and 23rd a tremendous hurricane struck the squadron, dismasting an scattering the ships; some ships, with heavy losses, reacher Mobile and others New Orleans and Campeche. For the third time an ominous destiny seemed to pursue Gálvez in the Gulf of Mexico.

Campbell, hearing of the disaster to the fleet and judging the occasion to be highly propitious, sent urgently an expedition from Pensacola to attack and take Mobile. At the front of the troops was Colonel Von Haxleden, with 60 men from the Waldeck Regiment, 100 men from the 60th Regiment, 250 men from the Pennsylvania and Maryland Royaltists and 300 Indian allies. The assault, by surprise and at night, took place on January 7, 1781. The small Spanish garrison, commanded by the young Lieutenant Ramón de Castro, valiantly repelled the attack by numerically superior forces and Mobile could not be recovered by the English. Colonel Waldeck, *«who led the action and was the best officer in Pensacola, a Sergeant-Major, an Adjutant, a Grenadier Captain and 16 soldiers died in the front ranks»*. The British expedition, now commanded by Captain Key, chose to withdraw. On the Spanish side there were 14 killed and 23 wounded.

into both Regiment, 250 men from the Pennsylvania and Maryland Provincials and 500 Indian allies. The assault by surprise and at night took place on January 7, 1781. The small Spanish garrison, commanded by the veteran lieutenant Ramón de Castro, valiantly repelled the attack by numerically superior forces and Mobile could not be recovered by the English. Colonel Wallace, carried off the action, and was the best officer in Pensacola. Sergeant Major, ... Grenadier Captain and 18 soldiers died in the front ranks. The British reaction now commanded by Captain Key, chose to withdraw. On the Spanish side there were 14 killed and 23 wounded

I ALONE

Gálvez was able to gather together the remains of his fleet and returned to Cuba, saddened, lamenting his bad luck, but not defeated. In Havana he proved again his firmess and character. Once more he appeared, time after time, before the War Board, begging pathetically for men and ships to attack Pensacola. Aware that a new and redoubled attack by Campbell on Mobile could cause to collapse like a house of cards all his previous conquests, he hammered implacably with his arguments at the dilatory tactics of the War Board:

«The English who sailed for Charleston were faced with a storm which scattered their squadron and took some of the ships almost to England. This is, more or less, what happened to us. But the English were not dismayed, regrouped, joined together and attacked with the fortunate result known to all of you. Are we not capable of as much? Has there disappeared that military virtue which was our characteristic in defeating the enemy? Have we so little constancy and tenacity in carrying out an enter-

111

prise that a simple tropical storm is enough to turn us aside? That will be the idea they will form of us, defeated by a simple blow, unless we are thinking of an objective of even greater importance. If this is so, I retract what I have said, because occupied in the nation's affairs I have sacrificed personal matters, as is my duty. I would be the first to desist in my efforts and look with satisfaction and without envy on the glories of another, but I fear that the decision will be for a program of lesser reach, for economy, for parsimony, and it, too, will be useless».

«Let us reflect for a long while on what we must decide. The King ordered the theater of war to be in America, and perhaps our compatriots in Europe, with less hope, may have won conquests and great successes, while we peacefully waste time which could be put to glorious use. At any moment peace may take us by surprise, and if this should happen, all the other branches of the service will celebrate the happy hour. But, we, men of arms, whom the King, after supporting us in peace, will have found us useless during the war. With what honor can we continue to wear a rusty sword which was not drawn when the occasion demanded?»

Gálvez's dramatic exposition managed to move the Board. But, although the decisive meeting took place on November 20, 1780, until well into 1781 the fleet was not ready to sail. At last, on February 13th, the fleet was at sea. And, on board, 1,315 men of different regiments. In the line, the warship *«San Ramón»*, commanded by Don José Calvo de Irazábal; the frigate *«Santa Clara»*, under Don Miguel de Alderete; the *«Santa Cecilia»,* with Don Miguel Goicoechea; the frigate *«Caimán»,* commanded by Don José Serrato, and the packet-boat *«San Gil»,* under Don José María Chacón, convoying the twenty transports carrying the troops. To these vessels must be added the four ships from Louisiana, among them the felucca *«Valenzuela»* and the barkentine *«Galveztown».* Gálvez, with his health broken, still convalescing from serious hemorrages he had just suffered, embarked in the *«San Ramón»* and, to avoid discord, assumed complete command of the expedition, including that of the squadron, in spite of which there soon appeared frictions and disagreements among the naval commanders.

After three hours the coast of Cuba disappeared and the fleet set its course for the continent. Gálvez, lost in thought, on the deck, seemed to scrutinize the horizon, recalling the unfortunate previous expeditions, when the wind and the storms destroyed his plans to wind up the Florida campaign with the capture of the key point which was still inaccessible to the Spaniards. But, now, the waters were calm in the Gulf of Mexico. Now, Gálvez was sure the opportunity would not escape him, that he would be able to finish off the great page of his life, whose final touch was there, beyond the foam which fringed the gulf, there where his eyes never ceased to look, in Pensacola. Left behind as distant as the faint outline of the coast, were the long months of arguments and disagreements, of inaction and delay, of opposed jurisdictions, perhaps secret envies and dislikes; but it had all passed, like a bad dream, and Gálvez was sailing again, ready to begin the game and risk triumph on the fall of a single card.

Nine days later a patrol of grenadiers and light infantry, with Gálvez at the head, landed on Santa Rosa Island, before Pensacola, and went on foot to Sigüenza Point, where at dawn they took seven prisoners. The English being warned, the fortress of Barrancas Coloradas and the two British frigates anchored in the harbor —«*Port Royal*» and «*Mentor*»— opened fire on the attackers. Gálvez ordered the emplacement of two artillery pieces and forced the two ships to withdraw out of range.

On March 11th the fleet weighed anchor to enter the bay, but the flagship «*San Ramón*» grounded on shoals and they had to work all night to get her off. Gálvez recommended to the chief of the squadron, Calvo de Irázabal, that he should send the rest of the ships ahead to avoid the blocking of the channel if the «*San Ramón*» ran aground again. The naval commander, backed by his officers, refused point-blank, judging the operation to be impracticable and opposing the entrance of the ships under the guns of the fort. Faced with this negative, and confronted openly by the two chiefs, Bernardo decided to force the entrance to the harbor with only the «*Galveztown*» and the «*Valenzuela*» which, as ships supplied by Louisiana, were under his orders, «*in the hope that the fleet might follow him*».

Gálvez sent to the «*San Ramón*» a message for Captain Calvo and a statement to the crew. He, himself, aboard his private barkentine, as an example, would enter the bay; whoever had the honor and courage to do so could follow him, *«because I will go first in the «Galveztown», to take away fear».*

Captain Calvo, beside himself, before the crew, declared that Gálvez was *«foolhardy and a gross upstart, a traitor to King and country»,* whom he would like to hang from the main-mast of his ship. Bernardo paid no attention to the words of the furious Calvo and, honoring his word, alone, without an officer or a soldier, raised the Admiral's flag on the *«Galveztown»* and, after ordering a salute of fifteen cannon, to demonstrate to all who was in command of the attack on Pensacola, raised sail and, defyimg the English artillery, which fired without cease on the barkentine, entered the road —followed by the *«Valenzuela»,* commanded by Captain Riaño— *«dropping anchor under the shelter of the Spanish cannon on Sigüenza Point, receiving the extraordinary applause of the army, which with continuous hurrahs showed the General their sympthy».* In a humorous gesture, the *«Galveztown»* saluted the enemy with fifteen salvos.

Their price hurt, the officers of the frigates asked Calvo to have the squadron follow Gálvez, but the commander was inflexible and once again ordered that no ship should move without his command. Only the next morning, pressured by all, and after receiving another message from Gálvez, he authorized the fleet to weigh anchor. In the afternoon, all the ships, with the exception of the *«San Ramón»,* filed through the channel, enduring for an hour the bombardment of the 140 pieces at Barrancas Coloradas. During the passage of the convoy, Gálvez, in a canoe, in a display of valor, in the center of the bombardment, cheered the passing of the ships and encouraged the crews. Once the ships were in the bay, considering his mission finished, delivered the squadron to Gálvez and, in the «San Ramón», which had stayed outside the harbor, returned to Havana. Gálvez reprimanded the officers for having obeyed the commander of the squadron, contravening his orders as supreme leader of the army, and they criticized him for having raised, arbitrarily, on his barkentine the insignia of Admiral, injuring the rights of the Navy.

Gálvez made ready to undertake the definitive assault on Pensacola. At the beginning of March he ordered Ezpeleta to come from Mobile with all the men available there, following by land the Perdido River route. Previously, he had sent Lieutenant-Colonel Pedro Piernas to New Orleans to mobilize all the forces in the capital of Louisiana, including the remains of the first invasion attempt broken op by the hurricane in the Gulf of Mexico, as well as the unit of 500 men which, under the command of Rada, had arrived late at the Battle of Mobile.

While waiting for these reinforcements to arrive, there began a correspondence between Gálvez and General Campbell, Governor of Pensacola, to guarantee the security of the population in the coming attack; they both agreed not to destroy the buildings and to respec the noncombatants.

However, days later, while the English spokesman was in the Spanish Camp; Campbell order the houses before the fort burned. Gálvez, angry, answered with this letter:

«Now that we are both making, reciprocally, the same propositions, as we are both trying to preserve the goods and properties of the people of Pensacola, I consider insulting on your part the burning of the houses in front of my encampment, on the other side of the bay, committed before my very eyes. This speaks of the bad faith with which you operate and write; although humanity is a word you repeat on paper, your heart does not know it, as your instructions are to gain time to complete the destruction of West Florida; I am indignant at my own credulity and with the noble manners with which you try to deceive me and because of this ó will not, nor should I desire to, hear any other proposition than that of surrender, assuring Your Excellency that, as I am not guilty, I will see Pensacola burn with the same indifference as I will see your cruel incendiaries fall in the ashes».

A new incident arose to try the patience of Gálvez. Three Spanish sailors who had managed to escape from the prison in Pensacola said that they had been ill-treated by their English jailors. Bernardo sent away Campbell's representative and refused to listed to any new propositions other than surrender.

At this time there came out to surrender to the Spaniards seven men who, taken prisoner in previous actions, had been set free by Gálvez after promising not to take up arms again on the English side and who found themselves in Pensacola. They were Colonel Dickson, Captain Alberti, Captain Miller, Lieutenant Bard, Boatswain Lowe, Doctor Grant and Armorer William Whissel; they were allowed to bring their families with them.

117

Gilberto de Saint-Maxent, and his son Maximiliano, officers of the New Orleans militia, took a courageous part in the operations at Pensacola. Furthermore, Gálvez's father-in-law helped to solve some financial problems of the expedition, advancing 6,000 pesos and making available in New Orleans, as a loan and without interest, a deposit of 60,000.

On the 22nd, as Gálvez had expected, there arrived by the Perdido River route, after a fatiguing march, the reinforcements from Mobile, led by Ezpeleta, and at nightfall on the 23rd there anchored in the harbor, without loss, the squadron from New Orleans which at Bernardo's urging, Pedro Piernas had raised, with a valuable reinforcement of 3,500 men. Two days later the troops moved from the island of Santa Rosa to the Mainland. Piernas brought highly pleasing news for the young Field-Marshal, his father, Don Matías de Gálvez, had just achieved important military victories, driving the English from the forts they held on the coasts of Honduras and Nicaragua.

The hour for the final assault on Pensacola was at hand. Campbell counted for the defense of the place, aside from his own army, on a great number of allied Indians from the Southeast. Warriors of the Creeks, Choctaws, Seminoles and Chickasaws, led by famous chiefs, such as the celebrated half-caste Alexander McGillivray, Benjamin James and Alexander Fraser, made this battle bloody and terrible, the result of which would have come sooner if the English had not had their help and the loss of life much less. Bloody attacks were unleashed by these tribes, and in one of them Gálvez himself was wounded. In the book by the North American writer John W. Caughey —«*Bernardo de Gálvez in Louisiana*»— is quoted the diary of Farmer, which noted in minute detail the daily attacks of the Indians and the scalps taken by them.

Immense joy broke out in the Spanish camp on April 19th when there was seen on the horizon a formation of more than 20 ships. It was soon identified as the squadron which had sailed from Cádiz, headed by the Commander-in-Chief Don José Solano, with several thousand veteran soldiers and the flower of the Spanish regiments —Soria, Hibernia, Cataluña, Flandes, Mallorca— under the orders of Field-Marshal Juan Manuel de Cajigal, with the best naval artillerymen and equipment in the fleet. In a few days here were brought in launches to the camp besieging Pensacola nearly 3,700 men. With the fleet there were four French frigates with another 725 soldiers. A real army, with more than 7,000 men, was at last under Gálvez's command, ready to put an end to the English presence in Florida.

Day after day, with the circle around the fort strengthened, the cannons thundered. Gálvez, to save lives in useless assault, dug tunnels and opened trenches, using his favorite tactic of placing batteries in unforeseen positions to threaten vulnerable points. At dawn on May 8th a shell struck the magazine of the Medialuna, which blew up spectacularly. Nearly a hundred defenders died in the explosion. Cajigal ordered the guns of the frigates to bombard the fortress simultaneously. Ezpeleta and Lieutenant-Colonel Girón launched light troops to exploit the success of the artillery. Gálvez then ordered a mass attack under the cannon fire. There was a ferocious hand-to-hand struggle, which lasted until General Campbell, judging his position to be desperate, raised the white flag announcing the surrender of Pensacola.

«To avoid new blood-shed, I propose to Your Excellency a cessation of hostilities and the drawing up of articles of surrender, as Your Excellency is disposed to accept honorable terms for the troops under my command, and for the protection and security which I might be able to provide for the civilians», said the message from General Campbell. On May 9th, the capitulations were signed by the Governor-General Peter Chester and General John Campbell. England delivered all the English forts and posts on the Gulf of Mexico, except for St. Augustine and the island of Jamaica; military honors were stipulated for the defeated, the conditions for their return to England and the guarantees offered to the noncambatant personnel, their families and goods.

The next day there formed up six companies of Grenadiers and the Chasseurs of the French Brigade. The English General marched out with his troops and after having surrendered the banners of the Waldeck Regiment and one of the artillery, they laid down their arms. Immediately two Spanish companies took possession of Fort George. The hard and bitter battle had lasted sixty days. There were taken 1,113 prisoners, not counting the blacks and innumerable Indians. Gálvez's army had 95 killed. The quantity of supplies, munitions and equipment captured was enormous.

In Havana, in New Orleans and in Madrid the bells pealed and there was a week of celebrations as a sign of joy at the victory. But, possibly, where the fall of Pensacola had the greatest effect was on the tired army of General Washington, which at last saw free of the English the Southeastern and Western frontiers. It was the greatest assistance the Americans ever received.

At the beginning of June all the prisoners had left in Spanish ships for Havana or New York. Gálvez left installed a provisional Governor and named to defend the place Commander Arturo O'Neill. Before leaving Pensacola he held a peace conference with the Indian tribes, in which he arranged and signed the terms of an agreement of alliance, trade and friendship which was not altered during the remain time of the Spanish presence in the province. Never again did the Indians rise against Spain in Florida and Louisiana.

The chapter of rewards was as ample as it was deserved for the man who, dominating the complete arc of the Gulf of Mexico, had achieved the moment of greatest Spanish expansion in America. Carlos III ordered that the name of Pensacola Bay be changed to that of Santa María de Gálvez; that the fort at Barrancas Coloradas should be named San Carlos, while Fort George should be called Fort San Miguel. Gálvez was promoted to Lieutenant-General and named Governor and Captain-General of Louisiana and Florida; his personal salary was raised to 10,000 pesos. In addition, and at the request of the inhabitants of Louisiana, the monarch created the County of Gálvez, with the previous Vice-County of

Galveztown. And, lastly, as the crown of his heroic gesture which made possible the conquest of Pensacola, Carlos III signed a Royal Order of November 12, 1781, of which Bernardo was informed by his uncle, José de Gálvez, in these lines: *«To perpetuate for all posterity the memory of the heroic action in which you alone forced the passage of the bay, you may place at the top of your coat-of-arms the barkentine «Galveztown» with the motto I ALONE...».*

REQUIEM IN TACUBAYA

The life of Bernardo was rushing to its end in a dizzying crescendo. After the victory at Pensacola, Gálvez moved to Cuba, on orders from General Don Victorio de Navia, an army of 10,000 men which, according to instructions from Madrid, should set out upon the conquest of Jamaica and Providence, the last English bastions in those seas. The plan consisted in attacking Jamaica from Guarico, on the Island of Santo Domingo, in a joint action with the allied French troops of Count De Grasse. Bernardo arrived in Guarico in February of 1782 to work with the French Admiral in the preparation of the campaign. A great disallusion awaited him. The fleet of Admiral De Grasse, with 36 ships, had been scattered by the English fleet, with 44 ships, commanded by Rodney, and De Grasse taken prisoner. It was necessary to put off the campaign against Jamaica and await reinforcements from Europe. In the meantime, there came the Treaty of Paris, on January 20, 1783, signed in Versailles by the Count of Aranda and the Duke of Manchester, which put an end to the conflict between England and Spain and France. George III of England ceded the two Floridas to Carlos III and officially recognized the United States. The Spanish field army was divided among Buenos Aires, Callao and the metropolis. With the peace, in April of the same year, the fleet of Admiral Hood arrived in Guarico with young Prince William, son of George III (the future William IV, the immediate predecessor on the throne of England of Queen Victoria), to whom Gálvez offered the freedom of the English prisoners taken in Louisiana. Days later, Bernardo embarked for the Peninsula with part of his troops, in the company of the veteran Captain-General Diego Navarro, after nearly ten years of uninterrupted service in America. In Guarico was born his only male child, Miguel.

Gálvez was able to enjoy only a few months rest in Spain, as in June of 1784 he is named as Governor and Captain-General of Cuba and Inspector General of veteran troops and organized militia of the Indies. But Gálvez continued to be irreplaceable in the affairs of Louisiana. Due to the signing of the Peace Treaty, on setting the borders, friction had risen with the Americans, above all, over navigation on the Mississippi, the right to which was claimed by both sides; the United States standing on a clause in the Treaty, and Spain on the fact that it held both sides of the river. To try to resolve this spiny problem there was sent to the new nation Don Diego de Gardoqui, as Chargé d'Affaires, with orders to wait in Havana to receive instructions from Gálvez. They held various meetings and Bernardo set out for Gardoqui the

Spanish reasoning on the problem: Spain held both banks of the Mississippi, by conquest, prior to the Treaty, which invalidated the American allegations. As far as the boundaries, those set on the 35th parallel instead of the 31st. Gálvez maintained contact with Gardoqui by means of a monthly courier, first from Havana and, later, from Veracruz. In one letter the Count of Gálvez told him to remind the government of North America of the services given by Spain to the United States in its struggle for independence *as the only rights they have on the Mississippi, but rights of gratitude towards us and not of usurpation. It, against all reason, they should make threats, ignore them, in the knowledge that we do not fear them as we have in the province sufficient veteran troops, a war-wise militia, the friedship of many Indian nations who dislike the Americans and more than enough experience in forest warfare*. The affair became progressively more bitter (Gálvez even reached the point of preparing an expedition in Veracruz to defend Louisiana) until there was signed in 1795 the Treaty between Spain and the United States. Later, in 1803, Carlos IV ceded the province to Napoleon, who sold it to United States.

Bernardo held the Captain-Generalcy of Cuba only a short time, as three months after taking possession of it, Carlos III appointed him to succeed his father, Don Matías de Gálvez, who had died shortly before, as Viceroy of New Spain. He was popular throughout America and Mexico received him in triumph. *Never was a Viceroy better received or acclaimed by every member of the public*. *His gallant, merry and gentlemanly attitude attracted unlimited benevolence»*, wrote the chroniclers. Mexico was suffering at the time from a disastrous food shortage due to the loss of the crops as a consequence of terrible frosts. They calculated the victims of that *«year of hunger»* at more than 300,000. Gálvez exhausted himself in helping the needy, distributing among them great sums from the funds of the Viceroyalty, subscriptions which he promoted, and, also, from his personal patrimony. He spent in these operations 12,000 pesos of his inheritance from his father and borrowed 100,000 more at interest. He went out, without protocol, to distribute with his own hands beans, rice or corn among the needy and constantly pressured the traders for food. Many people, driven by hunger, had moved from the country to the capital and were wandering the streets. Gálvez gave them lodging in the patios of the Palace, maintaning them at his own expense. Finally, he ordered the fields replanted with seeds supplied by the government.

To remedy the unemployment caused by the exodus from the villages, he intensified public works. To this measure Mexico owes the roads of La Piedad, San Antonio Abad and Vallejo. He opened higways, paved streets, began the construction of the towers of the Cathedral and, among other initiatives, distributed the vaccine against smallpox.

«He liked to look well and to be seen», states Valle Arizpe, Chronicler of the city of Mexico, and Orozco, for his part, writes: *«Gálvez was young and gallant; his profession as a soldier had made him frank and he had shown this in his dealings, ease and his little reserve,*

adding to his a merry character anxious for activity». He enjoyed, certainly, being with the people, having contact with them, strolling the streets and attending the spectacles. He brought foreign theatrical companies and famous singers to perform the latest novelties in the Coliseo. It was customary to see the Viceroy, accompanied by his wife, the elegant and charming María Feliciana de Saint-Maxent (who, as she had been born in New Orleans, the Mexicans called «la Francesita»), driving the fiery horses of their carriage along the Alameda or the Paseo de Bucareli, or strolling through the arcades of the Mercaderes or Las Flores, receiving the spontaneous acclamation of the passers-by.

On his taking possession of the Viceroyalty, the authorities organized a series of bullfights, which Gálvez, as a good Andalusian enjoyed greatly. When the people expected to see him occupy his box, or enter in a coach escorted by the Palace Guard, he appeared in the ring, with his wife, holdin the reins of a small carriage and driving around the ring, among the enthusiasm of the public. During the fights, answering the salutes of the fighters, he threw the matadors gold doubloons wrapped in silk handkerchiefs, which no Viceroy had ever done before. Once, *«such was his enthusiasm, he threw his own handkerchief, that of his wife and those of his children, and almost threw his uniform, which made for a joyous afternoon».* It was customary to have both Mexican and Spanish fighters on the bills. In the season of November, 1785, there were held in the capital of the Viceroyalty

20 fights, morning and afternoon; a woman even fought, to whom Gálvez gave 100 pesos for her art and skill. On another occasion, six women fought. After the fights there were all sorts of entertainments, such as greased poles, stilts, etc., and balloons were released —a popular fashion at the time— and, lastly, the people danced in the ring. A curious detail: it was Gálvez who introduced into Mexico coffee with sugared milk (which was drunk in France), and there was soon a commercial establishment to serve the public with this *«revolutionary»* innovation.

Without doubt to add to his popularity with the army, he ordered that his son Miguel, barely three years old, should have a place in the famous Zamora Regiment, celebrating this on the terraces and in the gardens of the Palace with a splendid festival in which he entertained, at his own expense, the officers and troops of the garrison of Mexico, while he presented his son in uniform.

One night he went, in his shirt, to put out a fire at the head of a group of halebardiers. Another day he donated his carriage to the Almighty because a priest, on foot, was carrying the viaticum to an ill person. He attended Mass in his private chapel, but he did not usually appear at the religious solemnities in the Cathedral. This was behind the appearance of an anonymous, ingenious and biting lampoon, of which the Mexicans were so fond, which reads:

> *«You are everywhere, I see,*
> *except in the Jubilee».*

Another referred to the inspector and adjutant of the Viceroy, the serious an energetic Don José de Ezpeleta, and his austere and acidulous wife:

> *«Te Viceroy, very good;*
> *His wife, the best;*
> *The Inspector, the Devil,*
> *And his wife, the worst!»*

Here, lastly, is another of these mural epigrams, dedicated to Gálvez himself, who the Mexicans knew from years before when he was in the country as Commanding General of the province of Sonora:

> *Y knew you little seed,*
> *before you were a melon,*
> *you handle well the baton*
> *and look after the «Francesita».*

Bernardo pushed the reconstruction of Chapultepec Castle, which his father, Don Matías de Gálvez, had wished to accomplish, and proposed to Carlos III that it should be here in the future that the Viceroys of Mexico should be received and given their symbolic baton, and not in the run-down old house of San Cristóbal Ecatepec, where the ceremony was now carried out. The King accepted the suggestion. However, Gálvez, instead of going ahead with the restoration of the fortress of the old Aztec Emperors, decided to build a new palace on the top of the hill, in the setting where there was a shrine dedicated to St. Francis Xavier, built in the days of the conquest on the spot where the Indian priests offered their sacrifices to the idols. From this, and from his desire to win at all costs popularity among the Mexicans, was born the dark rumor, spread by the bitter enemies of the Viceroy, that Bernardo planned to raise himself to the post of an independent sovereign in New Spain, placing a Gálvez dynasty on the throne. (Two hundred years before, in the same place, another Captain had been accused of a similar temptation, Hernán Cortés.) The absurd rumor appeared to reach, however, the knowledge of His Majesty and Don José de Gálvez was called to the Palace, to deny indignatly any such temptation. Such was the disgust of the veteran Minister of the Indies, above all at the thought the Monarch could have credited, even for an instant, such a calumnious suspicion that, according to the legend, it so undermined the health of the Marquis of Sonora that he shortly after died of a sudden illness in Aranjuez.

Many and true episodes in the life of the Count of Gálvez, in Mexico, have woven his golden legend. For example, the pardon he conceded to criminals condemned to death as *«thieves and murderers»* when he happened, *«accidentally»,* on the eve of Palm Sunday, to pass by the gallows where they were to be executed, in the place known as *«Egido de Concha»*. The Court in Madrid, informed by the Viceroy himself, acceded to the pardon given by Bernardo, but suggested that, in the future, he refrain from such decisions, recommending that he inform himself ahead of time of the place designated for executions.

On another occasion, while Gálvez was supervising the construction of a building, he heard in the distance persistent sobs. Intrigued, he found in the atrium of a nearby parish church several Indian women who were praying and sobbing. The Viceroy saw that these humble women were gathered around a corpse wrapped in a sheet. One of them explained that it was the body of her husband, which could not be buried because she had no money to pay the Vicar, who demanded his stipend in advance. The Viceroy sent for the priest immediately, who tried to excuse himself by saying he had not performed the funeral for lack of charity, but because he did not have the singers needed for the ceremony. Gálvez replied that he should dress himself at once, as there was no need for the singers, because he knew how to intone the service for the dead. Once the body was placed in the church, *«between the four tapers, the Viceroy, Don Bernardo de Gálvez, in his sonorous, strong and clear voice, sang the responses, which echoed through the vaults»*.

But Mexico was not good for the Gálvez family. His mandate as Viceroy was to be as short as that of his father's. A rapid and implacable illness lay in wait for him. On October 13, 1786, in the presence of Archbishop Núñez de Haro, the Dean of the Cathedral brought him the viaticum. To receive the Sacrament, Bernardo rose from his bed, against the advice of his physicians, and received it on his feet, wearing the uniform of a Lieutenant-General, with his sashes and decorations.

On November 30th, at daybreak, in the Palace of the Archbishop, in Tacubaya, to which he had been moved from Chapultepec, death came, at the age of forty, to the Malaguenian gentleman who had won at Pensacola a Castilian title, the audacious ally of the new-born United States, the Captain who had always guarded the lives of his soldiers, the *«friend of the Indian nations»*, the Governor, *«Christian, patient and liberal to the poor»*, to whom fortune had brought triumph —and death as well— while still in the bloom of youth. A saddened multitude pressed against the windows of the Palace, in the rain, praying through their tears.

Later, there rang out all the bells of the city while the cannon thundered their salutes. The body placed in the carriage, in uniform, accompanied by equerries bearing torches, and with the troops rendering honors, he made his last entrance into the capital. He had asked to be buried in the San Fernando Convent beside his father. The heart was placed beneath the altar of the Santos Reyes, in the Cathedral, at the request of his wife.

Two months later his posthumous daughter was born, who, in honor of the Patroness of the Mexicans, was named Guadalupe. The child, in memory of and gratitude to Bernardo de Gálvez, received the magnificent patronage of *«the most noble City of Mexico»*. The City Council *«made a gift to the widow of a pearl necklace with ten strands and long diamond ear-rings, and to the step-daughter a tortoise-shell chest, plated in gold, a diamond diadem and a large silver platter with a thousand escut-cheons»*. Days later, the widow, with her children, embarked for Spain, as Bernardo had recommended in his Will, in which there was also a mention of Macharavialla, the tiny place in far-off Málaga where his wings and dreams had sprouted, for which had fought, always with honor and hope, the energetic «Hawk of the Gálvez».

«When the fire burned most brightly», as says the verse of Manrique, the torch of Bernardo went out. It can be said that at almost the same time the power of the family was extinguished, as the Marquis of Sonora would survive him by only a year, dead in 1787. His other uncles had died previously. None of the three brothers —José, Antonio and Miguel— left direct descendants by the male line. Bernardo had a son, Miguel, who inherited his title, but died «a youth and single».

«They went down as they came up», says, as an epitaph for the Gálvez, an anonymous poet of the time:

> «The Gálvez melted away
> like salt in water,
> and like sparks from the forge
> they disappeared.
> They went down as they came up,
> like a sigh;
> May God forgive them,
> and may we not forget,
> that this world beats
> those to whom it gives adoration».

TWO HUNDRED YEARS LATER

After setting forth, in some detail, in the preceding lines the importance of Bernardo de Gálvez and the collective effort which he personified at a critical moment in the history of the United States, we return to our initial considerations and statements. If we ask ourselves, two hundred years later, in 1976, what is the American understanding and evaluation of the role played by Spain in the decisive chapter of the independence of their country, the answer is not, precisely, encouraging. The United States historians, in their great majority, judge the Spanish intervention in those events with a notorious lack of objectivity, considering it as a secondary function, lacking in importance and, of course, without any appreciable repercussion on the outcome of the struggle for freedom of the colonies. The military campaigns themselves in Louisiana and Florida, once hostilities had begun between Spain and England (and in spite of the capture of places of such strategic value as Manchak, Natchez and Baton Rouge, Mobile and Pensacola) are referred to as the «mini-

war» of Gálvez, because of the reduced area in which they were tought and for the short time in which they were achieved. On the other hand, there is silence as to the true volume of aid from Carlos III on the material level —money, arms, supplies—, in the diplomatic field and in the confrontation with the English naval forces in other seas and settings.

The willful comparison between the support given by Spain and France, so many times set forth, is not a fair argument given the different factors or interests at play in both nations in relation with the process of American independence. In the first place, France was then the first power in Europe and it is obvious that it was able to mobilize greater forces and more important military and financial aid. But, in addition, the interests of Paris and Madrid in that part of the world were sensibly different. France, with Canada lost and Louisiana ceded by Louis XV to Carlos III after the Seven Years War, had its hands free in America and no interpretation could be derived from its taking part in the Anglo-American conflict. France definitely sought in the new war a weakening of Great Britain which would allow it to maintain its dominant position in Europe, readjusting the international balance among the powers.

Spain, on the contrary, held extensive domains in the North, in the center and in the South of the continent, and its provinces, bordering on the United States, might find themselves affected, as was the case, by the appearance and influence of a new power arisen under the flag of independence and liberty. There was no lack of voices to sniff the winds of the future. A great statesman of the period, the Count of Aranda, in his clairvoyant exposition to Carlos III, prophesied in 1783: *«This Federal Republic was born a pygmy and needed the support of Spain and France to achieve independence. The day will come in which it will grow into a giant. Then it will forget the benefits received from the two powers and will think only of its own enlargement. The first step of the United States when independence has been won will be to seize the two Floridas... Then it will aspire to the conquest of New Spain».* Aranda knew, that with England eliminated, Spain would be left alone, face to face with the new American power. His prohesies turned out to be exact. And if he had lived another hundred years he would have seen, in 1898, how the United States definitely put an end to the Spanish presence on the continent which it had discovered and colonized.

In spite of all, in 1779, Spain declared war on the English and, in union with France, mobilized all its resources in an enormous and simultaneous effort in Europe and in America, with the sea as the principal theater of operations. Thus, a combined Spanish-French squadron, under the Count D'Orvilliers, entered the English Channel with 68 ships of the line and 400 transports with more than 40,000 men at the orders of General Luis de Córdoba. This formation neutralized in their bases important British naval contingents under the threat of an imminent invasion of the English coast.

This operation of diversion of forces was combined with the investment of Gibraltar. From 1779 to 1783 there stood before the Rock a French-Spanish fleet of 47 ships, 10 floating batteries and an army of 50,000 men at the orders of Don Antonio Barceló and Lieutenant-General Alvarez Sotomayor. These forces failed in their efforts to take the Rock, although they immobilized the English fleet of Admiral Rodney, who had 22 ships, 10 frigates and 200 transport craft. The essential objective of Spain on entering the war —the recovery of Gibraltar— was not achieved.

Meanwhile, the squadron under the command of Admiral Don José Solano, who aided Gálvez at the siege of Pensacola, joined with the French fleet of the Count of Guichén at the Island of Dominica in the Caribbean. Such was the powerful strategy employed at sea, in three different settings, to immobilize England and prevent its naval forces from sailing in mass to blockade the ports of the American coast and strangle the rebellion of the colonies. This Spanish contribution —with France— at sea, while the troops of Bernardo de Gálvez operated on the «second front» in Florida, constituted a decisive contribution, which has, however, been insufficiently evaluated in the general context of the war.

Some of the above can be attributed to a difference in receptivity of the philosophy and the men of the American revolution in France and Spain. It is true that the delegation from the American Congress, made up of Benjamin Franklin, Silas Deane and Arthur Lee, was welcomed with enthusiasm in a Paris already prepared ideologically by the spread of the works of Voltaire, Rousseau and Condorcet. The arrival of these men was an event and America became fashionable in Europe. The United States were the *«model people»: «a young people, recently sprung from Nature, devout, patriachal, with no passion other than that for the truth»*.

But neither in Spain was there any with holding of praise for the Americans and their struggle for the independence of their country, and the *«Gaceta»* published articles in their praise. Let us read what a Madrid periodical, *«El Mercurio histórico y político»*, wrote: *«The justice of their complaints and grievances, the accord and maturity which have reigned in their Congress, the spirit with which the colonists have managed to help those among their brothers who have suffered in the common cause, the virile effort with which they have shown themselves humanly resolved to face every danger before allowing their privileges to be revoked and, finally, with the attitude of the British Parliament, which has answered only with acts of authority, all appear to make respectable and sacred their resistance and just their pretensions»*.

Two centuries have passed since the American emancipation. During a period longer than this, for three centuries, Spain discovered, colonized and occupied more than half of the present territory of the United States, breaking the ground and placing its seal on enormous expanses. However, the Spanish traces have faded in the immense country. After the independence, and in spite of the Spanish participation in that enterprise, there was maintained the *«slogan»* inherited from the English which presented the Spanish as a cruel, reactionary and fanatic people, the old cliché which was used to *«justify»* the

139

plundering of 1898, and against which Walt Whitman reacted: «*To make up the future American identity, the Spanish character must supply some of the most necessary ingreients. No lineage provides a greater history in religious feeling and loyalty for its patriotism, valor, dignity, generosity and honor. It is time that we became aware that we will find no more cruelty, tyranny, superstition, etc., in the whole of Spanish history of the past than in the corresponding Anglo-Sazon history*».

Someone has asked, checking the indications, if the Spanish activity in North America was not useless. Some signs seem to confirm this. Such as this «*Columbus Day*» which takes away the Spanish quality of the Discovery. Even the Catholic roots in the United States are attributed to other peoples: Irish, Poles, Italians. And the Missions are presented as Franciscan, not Spanish. Will the effort to found cities, build churches and seed the virgin fields, cross the rivers and climb the mountains, to have fought at Mobile and Pensacola have been sterile?

The answers to these questions will have to be given by the future, but there are clear symptoms that the Spanish legacy in North America is tending to revive. A sign of this awakening is the language. The proportion of Spanish-speaking people in the United States, supported by the increasing Ibero-American emmigration and its high birth-rate, grows without cease and is reaching twenty million souls. Brooklyn, alone, has a «*Spanish*» population of 750,000. There are increasing, also, the Spanish Departments in the American universities, and the teachers of our language number in the tens of thousands.

Possibly the United States are marching towards a new, and as yet invisible, historical alternative. That of fully assuming in all its plenitude a geopolitical imperative which will push them to look, in solidarity and brotherhood, into their own continental area, towards the South, towards a reviving re-encounter with the Hispanic peoples, the only force which can give them a humanistic dynamism. Only then, will that past which we have called to mind not have been in vain. But this is an enigma whose solution will have to be revealed in this new century which is advancing on us implacably.

...Essay, the United States are inching towards a new... and as yet invisible historical alternative. That probably ...assuming in all its plenitude a geopolitical appearance which will push them to look at solidarity and broth... ...head into their own complexities, towards the south ...towards, revile the encounter with the Hispanic people... ...The only force which can give them a homogenistic dyna... ...unitas. Obviously that will that past with what we have called to ...ound not have gone to work). But this is an opportunity ... ...tion will have to be developed in this new century which ...tends us on us implacably.

BIBLIOGRAPHY

ALCAZAR MOLINA, Cayetano, *Los virreinatos españoles en el siglo XVIII.*

ANTIER, Jean-Jacques, *L'amiral De Grasses Vainqueur à la Chesapeake.*

BALLESTEROS GAIBROIS, Manuel, *España y la independencia de los Estados Unidos de América.*

BONEU, Fernando, *Don Gaspar de Portolá.*

BUCARELI Y URZUA, Antonio María, *La Administración de don Frey Antonio María Bucareli, virrey de México.*

CALDERON QUIJANO, José Antonio, *Los virreyes de Nueva España en el reinado de Carlos III.*

CAUGHEY, James W., *Bernardo de Gálvez in Louisiana.*

CAVO, Andrés, *Dos siglos de México.*

CONROTE, Manuel, *La intervención de España en la independencia de los Estados Unidos de la América del Norte.*

EZQUERRA, Ramón, *Gilberto de Saint-Maxent, a Colonial Patriot.*

FERNANDEZ DURO, Cesáreo, *Armada española.*

FERNANDEZ SHAW, Carlos, *Presencia de España en los Estados Unidos.*

GALVEZ, Bernardo, *Diario de las operaciones contra Pensacola.*

GARCIA, Casiano, *Aportación española a la historia de los Estados Unidos.*

GARRIGUES Y DIAZ CAÑABATE, Emilio, *Los españoles en la otra América.*

143

GIL MUNILLA, Octavio, *Participación de España en la génesis histórica de los Estados Unidos.*

GONZALEZ OBREGON, Luis, *México, viejo y anecdótico.*

HERNANDEZ SANCHEZ BARBA, Mario, *La última expansión española en América.*

MAUROIS, André, *Historia de los Estados Unidos.*

MORALES PADRON, F., *Participación de España en la independencia de los Estados Unidos.*

NAVARRO GARCIA, Luis, *Don José de Gálvez y la Comandancia General de las Provincias Interiores del Norte de la Nueva España.*

NAVARRO LATORRE, José, *Conspiración española.*

OROZCO Y BERRA, Manuel, *Historia de lo dominación española en México.*

PALOU, Francisco, *España misionera.*

PORRAS MUÑOZ, Guillermo, *Bernardo de Gálvez.*

PRIESTLEY, Herbert, *José de Gálvez, Visitor General of New Spain.*

RODRIGUEZ CASADO, Vicente, *Primeros años de dominio español en la Louisiana.*

RUBIO ARGÜELLES, Angeles: *Un ministro español de Carlos III.*

RUIZ GARCIA, Enrique, *Distrito portuario Matías de Gálvez.*

SOLANO COSTA, Fernando, *Los problemas diplomáticos en las fronteras de la Louisiana española.*

SOUVIRON, Sebastián, *Bernardo de Gálvez.*

TEJERA, Eduardo J., *La ayuda cubana a la lucha por la independencia norteamericana.*

THOMSON, Buchanan Parker, *Spanish Assistance in the War for North American Independence.*

VACA DE OSMA, José Antonio, *Intervención de España en la guerra de la independencia de los Estados Unidos.*

VALLE ARIZPE, Artemio de, *Virreyes y virreinas de la Nueva España.*

VAZQUEZ DE ACUÑA, Isidoro, *Historia de la casa de Gálvez y sus alianzas.*

YELA UTRILLA, Juan Francisco, *España ante la independencia de los Estados Unidos.*

ZABALA, Silvio, *Hispanoamérica septentrional y media.*

INDEX

© José Rodulfo Boeta
Edita: PUBLICACIONES ESPAÑOLAS
Portada y maqueta: VERDU
I. S. B. N.: 84-500-2156-1
D. L.: M. 26.663 - 1977
Printed by: I. G. Magerit, S. A. - Avda. de San Pablo, 47 - Coslada (Madrid)